Write and get paid for it

Terry Prone

POOLBEG

Also by Terry Prone

The Scattering of Mrs Blake and Other Related Matters
(Marion Boyars and Arlen House, 1986)

For Frank P. Rowan and Little Nephew

Terry Prone has been a journalist, magazine editor, broadcaster, scriptwriter and novelist, and is now Managing Director of Carr Communications, a training consultancy serving the international business community from its Dublin base. Carr Communications is also an industrial video production studio and a Public Relations agency. Terry Prone lives in Dublin with her husband, Tom Savage, and son Anton.

Contents

Chapter 1

Becoming a Writer

If a Writer has to rob his Mother he will not hesitate;
The Ode on a Grecian Urn is worth any number of Old
Ladies.

William Faulkner

- I want to be a writer, but nobody in my family ever had anything published.

- How could I cope with rejection slips?

- What do you do when you've always wanted to be a writer, but now you're too old to start?

- Before I try to become a writer, I figure I must be better educated than I am. Most writers go to university, don't they?

Let me tell you what this book is.

It's a sequel to a letter sent to a schoolgirl of 11 by a newspaper sub-editor of 50.

The schoolgirl was me. I had sent a few paragraphs about summer jobs to the Junior Page of a newspaper. Back came a letter:

Dear Terry,

Your handwriting is unreadable and you cannot spell.

Your piece, nonetheless, will be used on Saturday

1

next.

Learn to type. Learn to spell. Pay attention to what is cut out of the published piece. You could become a writer. Almost anybody can.

A hassled sub, who did not know me from a hole in the ground, gave me, free, gratis and for nothing, the best tutorial any writer could get. He also sent me a prize of a wristwatch which worked for a week. I kept it for ten years, just as I kept the letter, to remind me of two crucial things. Firstly, I had been published. (When rejection slips begin to arrive in tribal togetherness, you need to remind yourself that, as a writer, you have been publicly confirmed, even if it was only in the Junior Page of a newspaper.) Secondly, that there was no mystery to writing. No magical secret.

There *is* a secret to great writing. There is no book you can buy, no course you can attend, no method you can adopt which will make you a great writer. What *Write and Get Paid for It!* can do is help you become a published writer. You'll have to become a great writer on your own.

If you want to be a writer, you have a lot of competition. Inside almost everybody, there's a writer trying to get out. A number of people succeed. They join newspapers, become staffers on magazines, write scripts for radio programmes. They become freelances, pounding typewriters in their own homes, and in their own time, to make a living or part of a living. Or they have a novel accepted, and see it in hard-covered vulnerability on bookshop shelves waiting for purchasers.

For every would-be writer who makes it to publication, however, there are a dozen who don't. Their work stays unpublished, unread and uncelebrated.

Some fail because they write for the wrong markets, because the presentation of their material is unacceptable, or because they have not polished what they want to say so that it is suitable for publication. This book will help those who have had more than their fair share of rejection slips for such reasons.

It will not start those writers who cannot start themselves.

Some people who bubble with ideas never put pen to paper at all. The first time I produced a writer's guidebook, my mother read the proofs and went into spasm.

"You can't let them publish this," she said anxiously. "You're giving away all your secrets. Everybody else will get your places in newspapers and magazines."

She had a point. Except that from long years of running writer's training courses, I knew that out of every dozen committed, talented and increasingly skilful trainees, only two at most would ever make it as writers. The others would have occasional items published, but would never be able to drive themselves consistently to the typewriter and to the committal of words to paper.

Sometimes the problem is not lack of discipline or commitment. There are writers who do produce a manuscript, but then keep it in a bottom drawer, never daring to submit it to any publication or publisher. Would-be writers who rarely submit their work have a little voice in the back of their heads which suggests that they might suffer rejection. The little voice is usually right. Most writers have at least one patch of poor results, usually at the beginning of their career.

John D. MacDonald, the American thriller writer (*One Fearful Yellow Eye* and *The Scarlet Ruse*) produced 800,000 unsaleable words before his stories began to sell. However, by the time he died, on December 28, 1986, his name on a book automatically ensured that it would be a bestseller. From initial rejectability, he had achieved brand-name certain saleability.

When Rita Mae Brown wrote *Rubyfruit Jungle,* she found herself with a little-known publisher without a marketing budget to put behind the book:

Daughters Press published it in 1973 after every major hardcover house in New York turned it down. (Eat your hearts out. You all had your chance.) There was no publicity. Not one piddling ad. The book sold 70,000 copies. It was like a prairie fire. Bantam Books bought it from Daughters Press in

1977 and the book has sold millions of copies...

Nor do rejection slips confine themselves to the living. An American writer, maddened by refusals, not so long ago typed out the first chapter of a William Faulkner novel, plus an outline of the book, and sent it to twelve publishers. Seven of them rejected it outright, and only three spotted it for what it was.

Once you commit yourself to writing, then, whether you write what Herman Wouk calls a "great goddam doorstopper of a book" or an 800-word feature for a local paper, you are, by virtue of that commitment, open to rejection.

The point is that with practice, determination, a modicum of talent, and attention to your markets, you will see the flow of rejection slips diminish, and a satisfying proportion of acceptances dropping through your letter box. Paying attention to your markets means not sending something to the Pig Breeders' Weekly more suited to the Lingerie Newsletter, or a book about improving your sex life to a religious publisher, no matter what His Mischievous Portliness, G.K. Chesterton, says to the contrary.

Always remember that a rejection slip doesn't disqualify you as a writer forever. All it means is that one particular editor of one particular publication on one particular day did not think one specific piece you sent suited his or her needs.

Being a well established writer is no insurance against rejection. Sean O'Casey, one of the great names of literature, got a rejection from Playboy magazine in his later years. I interviewed his wife for a radio programme a couple of years after his death, and she told me that the experience had deeply depressed him. Fame and an assured place in the literary Establishment had not insulated him against the pain of rejection; they had, arguably, made him more sensitive to it.

The great difficulty about rejection slips is their timing. Prone's Law of the Rejection Slip holds that they never come except when you are depressed and poor, and then they come in sheaves.

But rejection slips are only one part of the problem. Being a

4

writer is like being a constantly spinning coin. Heads and tails follow each other endlessly. Heads you get published. Tails, you get criticised. Heads, you get famous. Tails you get beaten up in print for being famous. (Have a look at what happened to J.D. Salinger.) Heads, your book is turned into a film. Tails, they make sliced, marinaded nasties out of your theme. (Read William Goldman's marvellous saga *Confessions of a Screenwriter*).

- *Heads, your first book sells*

- Tails, the next book bombs—second books often do.

- *Heads, you are famous*

- Tails, your family quit talking to you because they see themselves in your writing and don't like the reflection.

- *Heads, you make money*

- Tails, not as much as your relatives, the taxman or you yourself thought you would. And the inflow dries up just as the outflows turn irrevocable.

If you are prepared for all of that, there are still endless reasons would-be writers use to put off the awful task of putting pen to paper or input to disk. There is, first of all, the obstacle of age. Which is, of course, no obstacle at all. At the younger end of things, the earlier you start the better. There are many newspapers and journals interested in young people's work. You can perfect your craft long before you leave school and build up a useful collection of published work by plying them with material.

There is no upper age-limit, either. Provided you don't get bogged down in an archaic style, there is no reason for an editor to whom you submit material to know whether you are sixteen or sixty. I know of one man who abandoned writing in his early twenties and returned to it only after retirement, who is now, in his seventies, making a tidy pension supplement by providing humorous pieces to newspapers and magazines.

If age is no bar to being a writer, education is no simple asset. Some writers, whether of fiction or non-fiction material, are highly qualified academics. Some dropped out of the educational system before they ever reached third level. There is no safe, predictable pattern. Indeed, the generally accepted patterns can be fraught with danger. Career counsellors, for example, often identify teenagers as likely journalists because they are 'good at English' and write a little poetry.

In fact, if you're putting your money on the teenager most likely to succeed as a journalist, pick the one who is not marvellous at English, but who has, instead, a talent for communal work on projects, or a capacity to organise thoughts logically and to meet deadlines. Many students, although they may have been regarded as topnotch in English in their teens, fail as journalists, because they cannot write simply or fast. Everything they touch comes out flowery, allusive, convoluted —and late.

Regardless of your educational achievements, what you must have, as a writer, is an understanding of what words mean and how they go together. That is usually developed by listening and by reading.

The only difficulty is that very few people listen. Watch someone being introduced to three guests at a party. Minutes later, the newcomer cannot recall the names of any of the three —because at the time of the introduction, the newcomer was firmly self-focused, and did not *listen*. One of the continuing problems of healthcare is what doctor's call 'lack of patient compliance.' Doctors tell patients what medicine to take, how frequently and at what times of the day, only to discover subsequently that a large number of those patients go home and swallow the medicines to quite different patterns. The reason? They did not hear the instructions adequately, because they were preoccupied at the time with their symptoms, the diagnosis or the price of copper on the futures market.

As a result, many people who would like to write lack the stored resources of good material which come about as the result of good listening. Long before Maeve Binchy produced her series of bestselling novels, she kept newspaper readers constantly entertained with columns based on conversations she overheard. When Maeve listens, she doesn't just listen for content or subject matter. She listens for the rhythms of speech, the phrases that distinguish one person from another, the idea that gets launched and lost.

The more you listen, the more you become aware that attracting and holding attention is not easy. You can buy guidebooks to help you find your way through the rules of grammar or to help you avoid lurking cliches, but if you cannot say what you mean in a way that someone else finds interesting then you cannot be a writer. Good writing is not a solo performance. It is a partnership with the reader. Good writing is not a monologue. It is a dialogue with a hidden auditor.

Too often, writers produce sustained monologues which are infinitely satisfying to the writer, but are of no interest to an editor, publisher or reader. Theoretically, the writer should be dead happy that he or she has reached his main audience, but this is rarely the case. Having written for their own delight, writers get startlingly resentful when their writing is not a source of delight to others.

When you put something in the post, you reach the point at which one of the major hurdles has to be overcome. That is the hurdle posed by the realisation that, for example, acceptance of your feature by the newspaper will mean publication of your name in that paper. For some writers, this can be an enormous problem, either because the are personally self-effacing or because they do not want their name associated with the particular topic being covered. The latter can happen when a writer who is known in one profession—a doctor, for instance, —wants to write a feature about something quite different, and is fearful that use of his name will be interpreted as inappropriate personal advertisement, or will skew the public's understanding of what they have written.

Before you submit something, work this problem out in your own mind. In nine cases out of ten, your real name is the best and least confusing option. In certain cases, it is acceptable to use a pseudonym. If you do not want anybody at the newspaper to know who you are, send a covering letter in the pseudonymous name. The covering letter is the one that introduces your article, gives your credentials for writing it, if you have any, and indicates any other relevant information.

If you have a sensible bank manager, the cheque (assuming your work is accepted) will be cashed for you without problems, even if made out to Simon Legree. Just don't try to dodge the income tax people by pretending to be unconnected to your pseudonym. They're on to that one.

I have eleven active pseudonyms, and am married to a man who uses five. At one stage, our postman, bringing a sack of mail addressed to several of these pseudonymous individuals, asked our next-door neighbour if our house was occupied by a commune. He was convinced that at least a dozen people were in residence, and found it difficult to believe that all of these names belonged to two writers.

Pseudonyms can be very useful when you fall out of favour with an editor. At one point in my own freelance career, a new editor took over a paper for which I had worked happily for several years, producing a couple of columns each week. When he started to make like a particularly pompous new broom, I resigned both columns and swept out of his office on a surge of self-righteousness which evaporated as soon as I got home and realised what the loss of the two columns would do to my weekly budget. Second thoughts drove me to the typewriter, where I inserted a new typeface, changed the margins and churned out two columns which I then submitted to my ex-editor under a pseudonym and from a different address. By return of post came a note of acceptance, and an expression of interest in running a couple of columns every week. What annoyed me in the short term was that he was willing to pay me more as a total stranger than he had been willing to pay the real me. What worried me in the long term was that he kept sending me warm encouraging letters, suggesting that a picture of me might be run alongside the columns and asking me to come in and see him so that we could have a face-to-face encounter.

However, for two years I kept up production of features and made excuses for non-appearance, and had a happy remote-control relationship with an editor I couldn't stand.

Pseudonyms allow you to make the most of the market, once you have broken into print. Making that breakthrough depends on your awareness of what publishers want to publish.

The simplest way to find out is to listen and read. Many would-be writers fail to do this, and send unsuitable material to editors out of ignorance. Later in this book, you will find specific guidance on writing for particular publications, but neither a tutor nor a writer's guidebook can substitute for personal awareness of what length of feature a particular publication favours, what layout preferences they have and how to meet them, and what subjects they are likely to cover. That personal awareness can only be achieved by reading extensively and making notes.

One of the disabling notions you must dispel is that all successful writers know all other writers and all editors and all agents. If you are without relatives/friends/contacts in publishing, this can give you a conviction that you are an outsider and that you will never break into the inner circle. Not so. It is never *easy* to break into print, whether in book or newspaper form, but if a worthwhile piece arrives on an editor's desk, he is unlikely to go around his office asking if anybody there is the writer's Uncle Bill. He'll just print it. Of course, a known contact in a magazine or newspaper helps. Being related to a writer helps. For example, by the time my son was eleven, he had seen three of his written pieces printed. All had been commissioned because he was the son of two writers. At his age, I had also had material published. But I had no inside track.

It's six of one, half a dozen of the other. Knowing somebody (or, like my son, being related to somebody) can get you past the first hurdle and make sure that you get published the first time. But it has the downside that people have a greater tendency to be critical of your material, on the basis that you would never have been published if you weren't so-and-so's son, daughter or wife. Getting past that first hurdle can be very difficult for a newcomer to writing, but the upside is that when an editor discovers you, he or she feels an enormous sense of personal pride and is likely to foster you and feel possessive in a very positive way, of the talent you personify.

Once you make a human contact in a publishing house or a newspaper, hang on to that human contact. Remember the name. Acknowledge the letter. Get the title right on your envelope and spell the name correctly. Keep their letters so that you know what they like and don't like. Try to solve their problems, and use their advice, if they offer any.

This book sets out to offer you a number of practical hints on writing and being published. Perhaps the single most important hint is: concentrate on possibilities, not on obstacles. People, notoriously, want to be writers, but want to avoid actually *writing*. Concentrating on the obstacles facing you is one sure way of letting yourself off the hook. If you face such insuperable obstacles, what's the point in trying?

The unavoidable truth emerging from virtually every writer's biography is that, if you have a passion to be published, and if you can produce publishable words, then, given time, persistence and professionalism, you will see your words in print.

While this book will concentrate in some detail on the selling of written material, on making money and on handling what money you make, I should confess, before we get to those details, that, for me, money is a pleasant side issue. I have made my living with words since I was a teenager, but I have never got used to the thrill of seeing those words in print, hearing a TV personality "ad lib" what I have written, observing actors putting flesh around my ideas or holding in my hand a collection of my words bound between two covers. There's no sensation in the world to match it.

But if you are to achieve that pleasure, if you are to justify the description "writer" on your passport, then, from the beginning, it's worth adopting 5 key Dos and 5 Don'ts:

DON'TS

- *Don't invent a mystique about writing to hide behind.*
  Writers write. And re-write. And cut. And submit. That's all there is to it.

- *Don't postpone writing.*
  Writing, like going on a diet, is infinitely postponable. You can put it off until next Monday. Or until January. Or avoid it until you leave your present job. You need to tell yourself that real writers write right *now*.

- *Don't let other writers frighten you.*
  If you want an excuse for not writing, the biographical paragraph on the inside back cover of any hardback or on the title page of a paperback will always provide one; other writers always seem more interesting, experienced and better qualified to write than you are. Be your own man or woman and get on with it.

- *Don't worry about rejection.*
  It happens. And when it happens to you, only you know or care about it. The letter arrives in the morning, and all day you meet people who don't know about this bad secret. Don't tell them, and don't concentrate on the negative; examine the submission and work out whether it can be improved or simply sent as it stands to a different market.

- *Don't worry about age.*
  Some writers achieve publication for the first time in their seventies. Some writers are *still* being published in their nineties. And some make it before they hit their teens.

DOS

- *Do listen.*
  Your own insights, feelings and experiences will inform your writing, but it must also be illuminated by the insights, feelings and experiences of others. Preferably expressed in their words, and with an indication of their facial

expressions.

- *Do concentrate on your strengths.*
  The old rule was "write about what you know about," but there are many writers, like Edgar Rice Burroughs, who have written about subjects they knew very little about. Science fiction writers invent the world they write about. In general, write about what you know about and write about what you care about.

- *Do think of your reader.*
  Readers are eager to be entertained, informed and stimulated. They hate being patronised, bored or forced to watch a writer flexing literary muscles in a self-serving way. Re-read everything you write, putting yourself in a reader's position, and when you feel boredom or irritation coming on, take your scissors to the material.

- *Do read.*
  Mark Twain said that the man who does not read great books has no advantage over the man who cannot read them. Writers need to read. Not necessarily just "great" books. They need to read a variety of books, so that they don't limit themselves to a single inescapable model whose work will over-influence their own.

- *Do be realistic.*
  Your first draft will not be perfect. But, because it *is* a first draft, you can tidy it up later. There is a lot to be said for the old writer's adage— "Don't get it right, get it written."

Chapter 2

Creating a Writer's Environment

It is a delicious thing to write, to be no longer yourself but to move in an entire universe of your own creating. Today, for instance, as man and woman, both lover and mistress, I rode in a forest on an autumn afternoon under the yellow leaves, and I was also the horses, the leaves, the wind, the words my people uttered, even the red sun that made them almost close their love-drowned eyes. When I brook over these marvellous pleasures I have enjoyed, I would be tempted to offer God a prayer of thanks if I knew he could hear me. Praised may he be for not creating me a cotton merchant, a vaudevillian, or a wit.

Gustave Flaubert

- How can I write when I have a family and limited space?

- Where do writers find the time?

- Setting up as a writer must cost a fortune?

- What do you do when you want to write but you feel too anxious or depressed?

All writers have a mental picture of the perfect writing environment. It's not always the same picture, but recurring specifications include:

- It must be peaceful. Ideally, a book-lined study with no intrusion of outside noise, but the capacity at any moment to open a window and hear birds trilling happily.

- It must be comfortable. Writers have favourite beds, desks, chairs, pillows, pens, telephones, open fires, cats and occasional bowls of goldfish, and without these favourites they feel less than comfortable.

- It must be free of financial pressure. No bills, no taxes, no dependents, no overdraft, no IOUs.

- It must be free of emotional pressure. No sick children, no alienated spouse, no complaining or aged parents, no critics, no deadlines and no enemies like editors or publishers.

- It must be stimulating. The air must be clear (unless the writer is a smoker, in which case a benign fog is preferred). The coffee must be fresh and constant in supply. The reference books must be ever-present. The music, if there is music, must serve as a creative catalyst. The by-standers must be admiring.

Each writer can add a few individual specifications to this general list, and even when it reaches its most exhaustive, it is not worth a damn. Celebrated writers and other publicly concerned figures have set up writers' refuges in many countries, where at least some of the specifications can be delivered. But every writer spending a month or more in such a refuge brings along a mental baggage of worries, hopes, concerns and preoccupations that are inescapable.

Most of us who write never get as far as a writers' refuge. We have to write in our own offices or bedrooms, and we have to learn to transcend our environment. Journalists learn quickly how to do this; a quick walk through the newsroom of any major newspaper boggles the mind of non-journalists, as they hear telephone calls, telex and FAX machines spewing out copy, television and radio programmes burbling out of monitors on the top of filing cabinets, typewriters pounding and instructions being shouted, and, against all of this cacophony, see journalists at their typewriters, concentrating on the task in hand as if they were in a monk's cell surrounded by total silence. You do not survive as a staff journalist if you cannot meet a deadline under the pressures provided by other people noisily meeting their deadlines at surrounding desks. In much the same way, if you work in an open plan office supplying scripts for a daily radio programme, you have no choice but to acquire the capacity to filter out distractions.

Time spent on seeking to create the perfect writer's environment is usually time wasted. Amazing feats of mental agility, creativity and practicality have occurred under the most adverse circumstances.

Perhaps the classic example is the case of a man named Williams, who, many decades ago, was in the US Armed Forces in America's Deep South. Williams was not your average malleable character. He lacked the subservience which makes lower ranks popular with officers. More pointedly, he tended to back-answer with profane clarity. By way of punishment, he was sentenced to a form of incarceration consisting of a box made of corrugated iron and measuring four foot cubed. This did not allow the prisoner to lie down, sit down comfortably or stand up, and ensured that, given the tropical heat, it was a matter of hours before he was in agony. The general pattern was for prisoners to beg for release at the end of the first day, and for truly obdurate prisoners to abase themselves in the interests of freedom within 36 hours.

At the end of the first day's incarceration, Williams's hot box was opened to allow water and food to be handed to him. Asked if he wanted to apologise for whatever crime had landed him there, he fixed the questioner with a look of silent contempt and was duly sealed up again. The following day, he sweated in the harsh darkness but again, at nightfall, refused to speak. Days moved into weeks, and eventually, when it became obvious to the Army authorities that he would die rather than give in, he was released. It took him some considerable time to learn to walk again. His fellow soldiers were vastly curious to learn how he had survived the torture and what he felt about the darkness and the heat and the enclosed rigidly defined space. He shrugged. It had required no great instinct for self-sacrifice, he indicated. He had been too busy to notice much of the misery. Too busy? Yes, he told them. He had been too busy planning the innards of a gun he had wanted to build for some time, and doing the mathematics of scale and placement. That work was now complete, thanks to the uninterrupted stay in the tiny prison, and he could have the gun manufactured at any time.

In due course, the gun was manufactured and became one of the long-term success stories of the arms trade. It was the carbine rifle, and its inventor was nicknamed Carbine Williams.

None of us would fancy trying to write a great novel under such circumstances; but it is worth pointing out that several works of literature have been produced under brutally restrictive circumstances. Solzhenitsyn "wrote" poetry and prose in the Gulag without always having paper on which to write down his drafts. He would think out several lines, and commit them to memory. The next day, he would tag further lines on to the base, learning the aggregate poem by rote. It was endlessly tedious and highly effective. Once released, he was able to transcribe from memory a considerable volume of stored material.

When Oscar Wilde was imprisoned in Reading Gaol following his disastrous libel action against Lord Queensberry, his imprisonment was a shattering blow, not merely as a constraint on his personal freedoms and an assault on his reputation, but as regards the day-to-day conditions in which he was kept. The oakum-picking hard labour and the health problems imprisonment developed in him were nothing compared to the impact of the shortage of reading and writing materials. He became so frantic for reading material that he developed, as he later told his friend Ada Leverson, a sad skill in reading other people's newspapers upside down. Writing materials were similarly restricted. Issued with a numbered page, he could fill that numbered page with his thoughts in prose or poetry, but he was then forced to relinquish it. There was no possibility of holding ten pages of, say, a poem. Within that constraint, Wilde wrote the anguished and unexpected *Ballad of Reading Gaol*.

The annals of imprisonment, of wartime, of illness and of deprivation are filled with writers who found the means to write and the internal capacity to transcend their environment.

Ireland's Christopher Nolan is the outstanding example. Speechless since birth and with only minimal control of his limbs, he writes by means of a "unicorn" attached to his head, his mother cradling his chin while he reaches every letter on a typewriter. One page takes a day's solid work for the two of them. Just how Christy Nolan keeps in his head the racing allusive sentences he creates, while engaged in the physically torturous placement of those words on paper, is a wonder to anybody who writes. But he does it, and the end result is marvellous cursive, award-winning evocative poetry and prose.

If you want to call yourself a writer, then you have to write, even when the wind is in the wrong direction, when the miseries are on you, the bailiffs are at the door and the bruises are turning from purple to dirty yellow. You cannot publish excuses.

But, assuming you have a family life and a career that keeps necessary bread on the table, how do you find the time to write? In picking writers' brains over the years, I have developed a list of methods, some of them verging on the philosophical, some of them brutally practical. Here they are, for what they're worth, in no particular order.

1 **Allocate time**
The tripwire is that marvellous phrase "I'll get around to it." Each of us has, in Yeats's words, "a little round of deeds and days," and a promise to get around to one's writing is virtually never fulfilled. The cares and riches and pleasures (mostly, it must be admitted, the cares) develop priority status and we never hit the target. If, however, you pick a time, whether it is half a day once a week, a weekend every month or, ideally, an hour or so every day, allocate that time

to writing, mark it in your diary, announce it to friends, co-workers and family as relevant, and stick to it, then you really *will* get around to it.

2 Give up something

Analyse your use of time and figure out the elements which could be excised. You may find, for instance, that you watch TV for two or three hours a night. Cut that time and you will be hard put to it, a year from now, to identify what you missed. But you will have no problem identifying what you gained.

3 Cut back on social life

Socialising is an important part of leisure time. It humanises us, softens some of the sharp edges, allows us to see perspectives different from the norm. It also takes up time, and if you can opt out of a regular evening in the pub, your friends will survive without you, your wallet will fatten and you will get more words onto paper.

4 Work on the way to work

This requires care, and cannot be done easily if you drive to work. But if there's a twenty five minute train journey between you and your job, then don't spend that time gazing out of the train window. If you share a car, then ask the other person not to talk to you, or invest in wax earplugs to keep out his companionship or the sound of the car radio. Most people waste transit time in daydreaming. Busy people who want to be writers cannot afford to lose that precious stretch of every day.

5 Work during lunch hour

Stay at your desk with a sandwich or an apple. Or find somewhere that will give you a fast bowl of soup and a table to yourself. Or go to the local park.

6 Work during slack periods

Every job has periods when activity drops off. The problem

is that this is usually when workers drop off, too. A teacher who has a free class can write in the staffroom. A Civil Servant who is awaiting the return of a document can write in the office. Someone caught between meetings with time to spare can write in the interval.

7 Buy time

Most of us, when we have an emergency, buy time or swop time. We ask friends to take over our kids. We arrange that our mother bosses around the painters. We brief co-workers to finish particular projects. We pay people to take care of our homes, cars or paperwork. Writers need to buy time by all of those methods. One tip, though. Do not tell any of the people you're seducing into helpfulness why you are asking their assistance. Nobody but you will think your writing is serious or important until your book hits the bestseller lists, so allow helpers to assume that some private problem requires three months (or six months, or nine months) of your undivided attention, but do not specify precisely what that private problem is.

8 Find simple ways to do things

It could be developing a standard letter with several applicable variations and empowering a secretary to decide which variation suits which recipient. It could be asking people to drop in to your office rather than travel to their office. It could be using duvets rather than sheets and blankets on the bed. But there are always ways of saving daily time. Shirley Conran's magnum opus (*Superwoman*) operated from a base assumption that "life is too short to stuff a mushroom." Each of us have time-absorbing things on which other people do not spend time. Writers in search of hours in which to write need to copy those other people.

9 Stay up later

This works if you are an "owl"; the sort of person who begins to surface at mid-day and who is bright-eyed and repellently bushy-tailed around about midnight. Owls can stay up later at night than "larks"—those people whose body clock dictates an early morning start. When children and spouses are abed and the television has died away to a white dot in the middle of the screen is as good a time as any to sit down in the warm quiet of the evening and begin to write.

10 Get up earlier

Novelist Bruce Arnold (*A Singer at the Wedding*) has been a journalist and art expert all his life. He gave up neither when he embarked upon the writing of his series of novels. Instead, he got up earlier in the morning, putting in several hours of fiction writing before he set off for the day job. The old saw about an early start and an early bed making people healthy, wealthy and wise has a lot going for it. Extensive research indicates that an hour's reduction in nightly sleep not only does not lead to a diminution in daily career performance, but tends to lead to a more optimistic and positive frame of mind.

Number 10 is my personal favourite of all of the time-creating options. Fifteen years ago, my partner began to present a radio review of daily papers which entailed his getting up at 4.30 in the morning and heading off to the studios. Initially as a gesture of marital solidarity, I got up at the same time and made breakfast. In the process, I discovered the obvious. Nobody telephones you or visits you at 5 in the morning. The hours between 5 and 9 are like virgin snow; pure, white, invitingly untouched, just awaiting your distinctive footprint.

I became addicted to early morning starts, and have kept more or less on schedule ever since. It plays hell with your social life, because if you go to a party you have an embarrassing tendency to put your head on the nearest shoulder and fall asleep. But it gives you wonderful dawn choruses in the summertime and a continuous sense, somewhat akin to the child's experience of mitching from school, of being one up on the world.

However, no matter what time you find to allocate to writing, it is important that you do not fool yourself. If you need to have a shower, clean your teeth, brew coffee and get a fire lit before you can commit yourself to the naked page, then you must allocate quite separate time to the achievement of all of these worthwhile objectives. An hour's writing time must be precisely that; an hour's writing time. No peripherals. No phone answering. No housecleaning. No research. No preparation. Just application of seat of pants to seat of chair and dedication to achievement of a certain number of words.

It is vital to set a target, but equally important to set a target to suit yourself. Some writers produce, after countless drafts and re-drafts, 250 words a day. Some writers produce 2,500. Under pressure, writers have produced original books or ghost-written material at a rate of up to 20,000 words a day. Your personal capacity and your concept of quality must dictate what word target you set yourself. But if you allow yourself to sit in front of a typewriter without getting something written, then you are not a writer, you are a thinker. Very important people, thinkers. But for the rest of us to benefit, it helps if they are writers who are eager to communicate, too.

There is a curiously disabling problem afflicting many writers, which is that as thoughts are placed on paper, they do not have the shining excitement they have, unexpressed, in the writer's head. Something gets lost *en route*.

That is a problem which is exacerbated, rather than solved, by postponement of the act of writing. A small dollop of personal experience may be worth mentioning here. Several years ago, my car and another man's car encountered each other with some speed and enthusiasm, head to head, fender to fender, on the open road. Both cars were reduced to scrap metal, and much the same could be said of the drivers.

Both survived. Both suffered considerable personal damage. In my case, the disarray was physically spectacular and mentally dizzying. First names no longer belonged to any specific individual. They drifted like particles of dust, to settle on any passing person. The name Anton, which belongs to my only son, free-floated and attached itself to my favourite (female) video director. My sister learned to answer to my husband's name.

This detached retina of my verbal skills extended to normal conversation, too. I would ask someone to make me a window when I wanted a cup of coffee, and indicate that it was time someone fastened the copier when I meant that a car door should be locked. My memory was like the vision of someone working up to a migraine attack; I knew that I knew something, but I could not quite reach it. So words, pictures and impressions went walkabout with me trundling heavily after them and only occasionally catching up with them.

Trying to write, against that background, was extraordinarily difficult. Words came in obstinately single units, instead of in dancing sentences. Non-writers, among them the doctors who were treating me, had no idea what I was talking about, and suggested that I lay off writing for a year or so, which is a little like telling a mainlining heroin addict that he should quit the hard stuff for ten days or a fortnight.

Instead, I set a target of 300 words a day and disgorged them turgidly. Six months later, the accumulated prose could have filled a highway-worth of potholes, and was unfit for any other purpose. A year later, formally precise prose was a possibility. Two years thereafter, the occasional felicitous phrase would emerge. Whenever it did, I did not kid myself that it was serendipity in action. It was cosmic payoff for daily hard labour, that's what it was.

A famous golfer was once complimented, after winning a tournament, on his good luck. He froze.

"Yeah," he said frostily. "I'm awful lucky. And you know what? The more I practise, the luckier I get!"

It's much the same with writing. The more regularly you force yourself to write, the easier writing will become. Now, let's be clear. Good writing is never easy. But it does get easier if you address yourself to the task as a routine part of your daily life. Wait for the Muse to descend upon you and you could be doddery by the time she/he/it does. If she/he/it EVER does. My personal view is that if I were a card-carrying Muse, I wouldn't

22

descend that frequently on people sitting around drinking Scotch on the rocks. I'd feel more called upon to visit some poor hardly-able who had been sitting at a typewriter every day of the week for three months looking miserable but willing.

Being in position when the Muse descends is a good idea. Having the tools of your trade to hand also helps. Even the most marvellous writing cannot reach a reader if it is not acceptably presented. If you outpour creatively using a ballpoint pen on lined paper, then no matter how good the quality of the outpouring, you have a problem. Nobody, today, wants to have to read handwritten manuscripts. Many publishers and editors do not have a burning desire to read any speculatively submitted manuscripts, but that is a later bridge to cross. For the moment, either get a typewriter or find someone who will type out your material for you. Typing services advertise themselves in newspapers, local shops and the classified telephone directory. It is always cheaper and usually more satisfactory, however, to do your own typing.

Second-hand typewriters are often on the market relatively cheaply, and as long as their innards are OK and the type-face undamaged, it does not matter how antiquated they look. On the other hand, an investment in a better quality typewriter is rarely money down the drain. As a freelance over a couple of decades, I consistently invested in typewriting technology which was just that little bit better than I could afford.

I got started on an extraordinary old typewriter that looked like a church organ and sounded like sustained artillery. It bit holes in the paper every time it had to type the letter "o", and I found myself trying to write features for newspapers without that letter in them. It was only later that I discovered that someone had produced an entire book without—if I remember rightly—the letter "e." The missing letter was the book's Unique Selling Proposition.

Next step for me was a portable. After that came my first electric typewriter; an odd little machine without a golfball, which at the time was state-of-the-art, but with bright green keys and a tendency to go on resentful strike if you accidentally hit two of the keys at the same time.

After that came a heavy duty electric machine which had endless typefaces. This capacity to change the look of a submitted manuscript I found very useful as a way of supplying lots of different kinds of materials to an editor who would have felt threatened by one over-active supplier. One day, he got a feature neatly typed with justified margins, using Victoria 10pt typeface. The following day, a feature arrived on Roma 12pt with unjustified right hand margins, and he never dreamed that the two came from the one writer.

The big breakthrough was the word processor. The people who had supplied the heavy duty machine arrived one day, telling me that for an astonishingly small outlay I could have full word-processing facilities. I did not know what this meant, and the clarification left me mystified at a higher technological level. They then swore to me that this was the machine Len Deighton used every day of his life. I figured that if there was such a thing as guilt by association, there might be a parallel possibility, loosely entitled Talent by Technological Reference, and told them to leave Len Deighton's sister machine plugged into my existing machine for a week.

During that week, I discovered that here was a device which let you look at what you had written it before you fed it out, allowed you to correct typing and other mistakes, permitted you to move paragraphs around within the text, facilitated you in your thieving of a quotation from one feature into another, and alerted you to over-use of a particular word or phrase. A word processor, I found, told you how many words you had produced in a morning's work, kept everything you produced in a file so that, at the touch of a button, you could look at what you wrote six months previously, and allowed you radically to improve the physical presentation of your writing. I hocked my inheritance and bought the word processor.

It turned me into a technology freak. I now have a lap-top WP which I carry around with me. This explains the gorilla-like length of my arms; the machine weighs 14 pounds, which looks light in an advertisement and feels heavy on a long journey. I have meaningful relationships with FAXes, dictaphones, modems and mouses. Writers do not have to be surrounded by sophisticated keypads, but if you want to make a living as a writer, then you should invest in the tools of your trade, and concentrate at least some of your energies on making your work look good.

Learning to type is easier than it sounds. There are countless training methods available which will give you a basic grasp of the skill. Speed follows with practice. When it does, you may find that you write more quickly and easily by using a typewriter than by initially writing by hand; it is possible to type and think at the same pace, whereas handwriting tends to be slower than thought processes, and so you can lose fast-fleeting insights and images.

Whatever kind of typewriter you use should be made to work for you. Use good white paper, leave large margins, treble-space your lines and employ a ribbon which is not worn down to its component threads. Learn to identify when you are close to the end of a page, so that you do not have to hold the paper in the machine while you complete typing the last line.

An old typist's trick is to put a tiny pencilled X about an inch and a half from the bottom. When that appears on your line of type, you know you have to finish the sentence you're on and not embark on another.

Unless you produce an extraordinary volume of text, you are unlikely to need a photocopier, but no manuscript should leave your hands before there is a copy in your files. Never rely on the files of a word processor for this purpose. A word processor can "crash" taking your work with it. Prevent this disaster by feeding out an extra hard copy and storing it carefully, or by photocopying the original before mailing. Carbon copies are useful records, but should never be sent to editors; they clearly indicate to an experienced editor that what is being submitted is a second version, and raise the question of what happened to the first version.

The precise shape manuscripts should be for different markets will be discussed later in this book. Suffice it to say here that although editors tend to deny being influenced by superficialities such as the appearance of a manuscript, the reality is that a text which looks reasonably easy to read is much more likely to get immediate attention than one closely typed with miserable margins on slimy grey paper using a typewriter ribbon pale with age and scrunched into an envelope so small as to have given the manuscript a terminal case of the bends.

Investing in a typewriter and good quality paper is not the end of your outgoings. If you plan to write for newspapers or magazines, then you have to buy newspapers or magazines. Obvious? Not so. I am fascinated, when I run writing courses, to find students who are absolutely determined, for example, to get a column into a woman's magazine, but who have not recently bought a woman's magazine. There are writers who produce a feature and decide, off the top of their head, that it should fit the needs of a national newspaper, without reading the feature pages of the national newspaper to find out whether the publication takes material in the 6,000 word category. Very few do.

Buying newspapers and magazines can be expensive, which is one of the reasons you must keep accounts of what you purchase in the way of writer's duty. Later in this book, you will find information about book-keeping and accounting. However, at this point it is worth stating bluntly that *whatever* you buy to help you write, whether that be a pen, a typewriter, several magazines, a stand for holding reference books, a recorder, a bottle of typewriter eraser fluid or a box of paper clips, should be noted as part of your expenses, and the receipt kept for income tax purposes. Think professionally from the very beginning. Ignore the vaporous little voice in the back of your mind which suggests to you that real writers don't think of things like income tax and expenses. Real writers are humans who need to eat, drink and be a bit merry. All of which costs money. Real writers no longer live in garrets and think great uncostly thoughts. They have to deal with bank managers who are deeply suspicious of anybody whose main asset is something as intangible as ideas. They have to cope with illness and inflation. They have dependents to support and rents to pay. They need to set up simple structures so that neither the getting nor the spending of money becomes a daily preoccupation. If the systems are in place, the writer need waste no time on them. He or she can get on with writing.

Another inevitable expense is reference books. (On page 196, you will find a sample list of reference books worth buying.) Writers need libraries, so that for leisure or ideas-refreshment, they can dip into the depths and shallows of other writers' minds. More practically, they need to build up reference libraries or have ready access to them. Initially, in your own home, you need a good dictionary and the humility to use it regularly. Most people do not have that humility. As a result, they use "prevaricate" when they mean "procrastinate" or "flaunt" when they mean "flout." One political speech I edited recently suggested that it was "encumbered" upon Government to take a particular course of action. What the writer actually meant was that it was "incumbent," although he had inadvertently hit a vein of humour which, sadly, went unexplored.

Other books worth having are the *Writer's and Artist's Yearbook*, which comes out annually (published by A. & C. Black, Ltd). This covers everything from writing for newspapers to your rights as a writer. Never, ever lend your copy of *Writer's and Artist's Yearbook*, to someone else—you will never get it back, and it is one of those books you can go back to again and again.

Quite apart from not lending this volume, I have a personal prejudice about book borrowers which finds expression in my diary, where I note who borrows what, and pursue the borrowers of particularly precious books relentlessly. My boss once borrowed Thomas Kennealy's *Three Cheers for the Paraclete* and it took me seven years to get it back. It was not in print at the time, so I could not simply replace it.

The lack of a library of reference books never holds back someone with a burning urge to put pen to paper. The essential point is that buying books can help smooth a couple of edges here and there. Reference books should not be allowed to distract you from the overriding importance of getting words down on paper. When you are writing a feature about aspirin, and you look up the story of the German inventor, the little entry at the end of the page which directs you to other relevant material is extremely tempting, and very dangerous. You can end up spending a day reading everything about the research, development and marketing of pharmaceuticals, rather than writing your interesting piece about the painkiller.

A potent time-waster—and my personal *bete noir* is a good dictionary of quotations. You go to one of these volumes for a quotation about elections, because a general election has just been called and you figure somebody, somewhere, at some stage said something quotable about elections. First problem is that under Elections is a blank space, decorated only with the suggestion that you should look under Voting. You look under Voting as instructed, and there are three pages of quotations. Some of the best of them are from people who may once have been household names, but are no longer even outhousehold names. You waste time figuring whether you should use their comments, or will their present obscurity rob the quote of impact.

You weigh up Adlai Stevenson ("The idea that you can merchandise candidates for high office like breakfast cereal — that you can gather votes like box tops— is, I think, the ultimate indignity to the democratic process.") against George Bernard Shaw ("An election is a moral horror, as bad as a battle except for the blood; a mud bath for every soul concerned in it."). Then it strikes you that you might usefully peruse the sections devoted to Citizens, Democracy, Government or Politics and Politicians. Two hours later you have perused yourself stupid and there are still no words on your piece of paper. Never be dominated by research, whether conducted by yourself or handed to you in condensed, reference-book form. The main job —to introduce new ideas or to re-introduce old ideas—is yours, and you must not hide behind acres of references, however tempting it may be. One writer on theatrical subjects years ago greatly irritated a number of actors in a large repertory theatre by this self-protective habit. One night, a large sheet of virgin white paper appeared on the notice board in the greenroom. When you got close to it, you noticed that there was tiny handwriting in the lower right hand corner. The handwriting said "This is X's weekly feature without the quotations."

Investing in your future as a writer inevitably brings up the question of education or training. If you are in your teens when you have happened on this book, then you face choices about further education. Will you go to university and do an Arts degree or will you do a Media Diploma in a specialist college or will you fling yourself, academically unshod, upon the labour market to learn by doing?

The buck stops with you. Some writers have encountered a brilliant professor or tutor in university who has freed all of their communications potential and developed a writer out of an ambition. Some writers have found the same kind of stimulus in a specialist college and swear by the more specific skills imparted in such colleges. Some writers sneer at higher education considering it a method of learning, the mechanics of literary criticism rather than the rudiments of writing.

I have yet to put my hand on objective research which establishes the single best path to success through education. All writers swear by the method by which they achieved success, assuming they DID achieve success, but the fact is that there are many routes and that what is successful for one individual at one time is a sure recipe for failure in the case of another person at a different time.

What every novice should be wary of are commercial writing courses which are advertised as having astonishing success rates. Even when these success rates are legally defensible, they are rarely valid for personal extrapolation. Let me give you an example. In 1988, during the summer, I ran a fortnight's course which involved four participants, giving them the sketchiest of introductions to basic media skills. One of the exercises involved putting them in a TV studio to interview a well-known figure for half an hour. Two of the participants interviewed a novelist and radio personality. The object of the exercise was to keep alive in a television studio for the first time, to ask questions and fill half an hour with reasonably interesting material. For people who had never done a half hour interview before, that was a major task, and succeeding was a major achievement.

As soon as the interviews were complete and the author/radio personality had departed, both interviewers were told "OK, good enough so far. Now sit down, both of you, and write personality profiles (see page 77) on the man you've just interviewed, using quotations from the recording that was made." Now frankly exhausted and resentful, both sat down to an extra task. When the profiles were complete, they were told to market them. Within three weeks, both had been published. A fabulous success story? Absolutely. Except that very little credit accrues to the training in this instance. Firstly, the two interviewers were, in quite different ways, unusually talented. Secondly, both had made a decision to change career in the short, rather than the long term. Thirdly, both were on holiday and undistracted by normal work.

It also happened that the man they interviewed was unusually open and frank about his successes and failures. More to the point, his critically-acclaimed novel was due for issue in paperback two weeks after the interview in studio, although journalists were not generally aware of the fact. The end result was a success rate from a single, small, introductory course that might lead to unrealistically optimistic expectations of subsequent courses.

Whenever you see or hear claims for writing courses, bear that in mind. No course makes writers out of non-writers. What some courses do is provide talented people with the structural guidelines within which their talent can find adequate expression. What other courses do is remove the mystery from writing, so that people waiting in the wings of their own talent are suddenly freed to move into the spotlight and start performing. What still more courses do is provide enough stimulus to get short term success for writers who, when the course finishes, cannot continue to produce saleable material without the moral support of constructive criticism, the group dynamic provided by the shared educational experience and the artificial pressure of deadlines and expectant tutors.

Not all correspondence courses are a waste of money, despite the celebrated exposes of a decade or so back, where American brand-name correspondence courses were revealed as being shoddy at best and nakedly exploitative at worst. But if you have more money than self-confidence, you are fair game for a number of training courses of limited real value. You know the kind of course. The kind where the advance advertising says something like "We are looking for Poems to Publish." Except that before they buy a poem from you they think you should sign up for a four- month course.

There is no single course that will equip you to be a writer. What a course *can* provide is attention and encouragement and a little helpful guidance. It's surprising how rarely those three things are available freely to new writers from someone with a little credibility. Attention is difficult to get in a busy world. Encouragement too often has to be paid for. Helpful guidance is not easily accessible if you don't come from a family with a tradition of writing.

That is not to say that you cannot develop a guardian angel. It does not have to be someone who is a writer himself. One of the people I have exploited most successfully down the years as a first reader of draft material is not a writer. She is a person who likes reading. She is a reader with a low boredom threshold, strong views and no hesitation at all about expressing them. She also wants me to write as well as I can possibly write. Every home should have one...

Horror writer Stephen King has a quite different approach to eliciting advice and seeking mentors.

> Show your piece to a number of people—ten, let us say.
> Listen carefully to what they tell you. Smile and nod a lot.
> Then review what was said very carefully. If your critics
> are all telling you the same thing, about some facet of your

story—a plot twist that doesn't work, a character who
rings false, stilted narrative or half a dozen other
possibilities—change that facet. It doesn't matter if you
really liked that twist or that character; if a lot of people
are telling you something is wrong with your piece, it is. If
seven or eight of them are hitting on that same thing, I'd
still suggest changing it. But if everyone—or even most
everyone—is criticizing something different, you can
safely disregard what all of them say.

Having a mentor or supportive critic or confidant is a help. But
no more than that. Don't ever fall into the habit of talking about
your work rather than working.

It doesn't matter than you have had your soul enlarged by
editorial discussion. What matters is the quantity and quality of
words that have found a home on your nice thick white paper.

Ultimately, being a writer is a lonely experience. You're on
your own, and it therefore behoves you to take care of your key
asset: yourself. One of the most dangerous myths about writers
is that they tend to poor health or to the active propagation of
poor health or that they dangerously neglect their health to
pursue their art. We were all nurtured on stories of poets
frantically pouring out their felicities before death o'ertook
them, on tales of consumptive women flushed with fever and
fast-ebbing creativity. The great wars added their contributary
details of writers dying in the trenches and being buried in one
small corner of a foreign field. The De Quincy-launched saga of
the drug-taking scribe dreaming dreams and seeing visions was
developed by the Alistair Crowleys and Timothy Learys. The
brilliant alcoholic writer became an inevitability of literary life
as a result of men like Scott Fitzgerald, Dylan Thomas and
Brendan Behan.

You don't have to be sick to be a writer. While chemical
ingestion or alcohol consumption may appear to aid creativity
in the short term, in the long term both are the road to notown.

Writing, especially part-time writing, is a demanding career,
which requires considerable stamina. Regular sleep, regular
exercise, no smoking, a good chair and frequent walkabout

breaks during long writing stints are all worthwhile. The flip side of all of this physical positive thinking, I have to admit, is that writing is one of the few jobs you can often continue to do when bed-ridden, bedraggled, rotten with viruses or bacteria, clinking with broken bones or fifty pounds overweight.

In creating a writer's environment for yourself,

- *Do* create time, even if it means cutting out things you enjoy, like sleeping.

- *Do* create peace for yourself, even if it means calling a summit conference of friends and family to state your need for total peace and isolation at particular times.

- *Do* go to a writer's refuge if you get the chance. But don't expect it to turn you into Jane Austen in a couple of tranquil weeks.

- *Do* set a target and keep to it.

- *Do* invest in reference books over a period of time—and don't allow them to become time-wasters for you.

On the other hand,

- *Don't* postpone writing until you have established perfect working conditions. The given reality is always less than perfect, but you have to live with it.

- *Don't* say "I'll get around to writing." No, you won't.

- *Don't* believe that correspondence courses or evening classes will transform you into a writer. They can help, marginally, and at a cost.

- *Don't* kid yourself about what constitutes real work.

- *Don't* be mean about paper, time or equipment. Cut back on food, fun or furs, but get your priorities right.

Chapter 3

Freelance Journalism

Writing is easy. All you do is stare at a blank sheet of paper
until drops of blood form on your forehead.

Gene Fowler

- What exactly is a freelance journalist?

- Can you make a living at it?

- Where do you start?

- Don't freelances feel very isolated without the support of
other writers, such as you would have in a staff job?

There are a lot of good reasons why people who think of
themselves as Writers should occasionally slum it with the rest
of us, and produce words for newspapers, magazines, TV or
radio programme. For one thing, there's usually a deadline, and
a deadline, like the prospect of being hanged in the morning,
concentrates the mind wonderfully. For another, there's
payment, which can keep life in the body while the Great Novel/
Epic/Theatrical Trilogy is in the lengthy process of creation.

Talk about journalism to a group of people who think of
themselves as serious writers (or as potentially serious writers)
and what you get is a brisk exchange of prejudices. Words like
"shallow" and "sensationalist" are proffered to justify their
refusal to become involved. Where someone overcomes their

prejudices and decides to have a bash at the journalistic end of writing, the portents are positive. All of us who are journalists would like to believe that we form an elite profession equipped with valuable specific skills, but the reality is that many of us started off in other jobs, with other skills and interests and learned, often by trial and error, how to be journalists.

The real hurdle is the first piece of copy to be written and submitted. Someone used to writing short stories, longer fiction or poetry needs to have a system in order to produce worthwhile journalism.

The system could take the form of a grid

What do I want to say?	**Who** to?	**How** can I say it?	**What** should I not say?

The extreme left hand column of the grid establishes the subject matter of the feature or article. Too many people start to write before they have clarified their purpose and the points they plan to make. A general statement of what topic is to be explored is not enough for that left hand column. Into it also need to go the main points the feature will cover. The number will vary, but for a thousand-word space, fewer than three main points would result in a rather thin feature, whereas ten main points would create unreadable density.

Having established what you want to say, the next thing is to work out who you're going to talk to. The target audience. The imagined reader. The ideal recipient. Here is where writers should take a leaf out of advertisers' books. If you're planning to advertise a new cocktail that utilises only vintage brandy, the media in which you'll advertise it suggest themselves very quickly. You'll flaunt it only in media which are read/viewed by adults with a fair amount of discretionary income at their disposal. Similarly, once you have worked out who might be interested in what you have to say, it is relatively easy to work out which publication will best reach that audience. Some topics reach audiences most effectively through the variety pages of evening papers. Some through women's magazines. Some through the feature pages of the more substantial Sunday newspapers. Whichever is chosen instantly provides its own style constraints, criteria and length specifications. On the matter of length, one Sunday newspaper may regularly print features running to two and a half thousand words, whereas an evening paper may regard a feature of four hundred words as pushing at the limits.

Visualising your reader helps you to address that reader in the right tone. Queen Victoria said she hated Gladstone because he addressed her as if she was a public meeting. A reader does not like to be addressed as if he were a cross section of a vast public. Ideally, the feeling is of one person passing on ideas and information to another.

The third column of the grid is headed **How do I want to say it?** What that means is that the writer looks at the points he or she wants to make (Column One) and works out how best to express them so that they are easily understood and can be remembered without effort on the part of the reader. Making points understandable and retainable involves providing specific clear illustrations and examples for each concept. Every point in the first left hand column of the grid needs to be subjected to that discipline. It is important to think from the audience's point of view rather than your own, so the examples should be chosen from widely-shared experiences. Just because you have spent three months on a yak in Korea does not mean it is a good idea to liken travelling in a badly sprung bus to travelling on a yak. The reader may be totally stymied, rather than enlightened, by the simile.

You should also use this guideline to establish the tone of the feature. Are you going to be deadly serious and informative, or funny and provocative? Quite often, features fail because there is confusion here. The writer at one stage is a silent partner, unassertive, hidden in the shadows, and two paragraphs later is leaping around the page shouting personal opinions. Or the writer is initially your friendly local pundit, advancing chunks of wisdom and up-to-date information, and the next minute is getting facetious and jokey. The reader needs to know where the writer is coming from, and readers find major shifts in persona unsettling. If you are the mother of the bride, we do not expect you to dance naked with a rose in your teeth on the table at the wedding. Decide on your tone for each feature and stick to it. This does not mean that you cannot use an *unexpected* tone. One of the first regular newspaper jobs I got was when Mary Kenny, then a features editor on a daily paper, rang me up and suggested that I might become her fashion and beauty correspondent.

I gazed at myself in a mirror over the telephone. Four stone overweight, dressed in clothes you would flatter by suggesting they had seen better days, and as innocent of the currently favoured designers as an Aboriginal in mid-walkabout.

"Mary, I'd love the job and I could do with the money," I said timidly. "But I don't know anything about fashion and beauty."

"No problem," came the reply. "I don't need you to *know* anything. I need you to be funny."

Her position was that she had to have regular features on fashion and beauty, because they were mainstays of women's pages then, as, fifteen years later, they still are. But she believed that they tended to be dull (earnest discussions of what colours are acceptable this quarter) repetitive (count the number of times, during a fashion collection season, that newspapers use the headline 'The Long and The Short Of It' to deal with fluctuating hemlines) and unappealing except in terms of their pictures. Beauty features, too, were often little more than filler text around a picture of a pretty face, with a few eternal verities from the cosmetics industry thrown in, chief of those verities being 'cleanse, tone and moisturise.'

Mary Kenny's brief was deceptively simple. She wanted fashion and beauty angled so that they were a constant surprise. What she did *not* want was a newsy beginning to a feature, then a sudden burst of comedy, and finally a diatribe about the sinful wastefulness of contemporary addiction to designer labels. She wanted, as do most editors, a distinctive and internally coherent writer's tone in each column.

Having, then, identified the tone you're going to use in writing the piece, you move on across the grid. The final column is **What should I not say?** In business training courses, they call this exercise 'Prioritising.' In journalism, we call it editing.

Editing should start long before you submit your feature to an editor. It should start on your first draft. Anything that does not contribute to the onward movement of your feature should go. Anything that moves off at a slight tangent should go. Anything that is just a personal opinion and casts no general light on the subject should go, unless the feature is a personal experience piece based on life as she is lived in your home. This editing and re-write process generally results in a shorter feature, which is a positive factor in marketing terms. Relatively few publications operate on a 'never mind the quality, feel the length' basis, and some actively prefer brevity and concision. Cutting the fat from a feature always improves it.

At a certain point, though, the editing and re-writing process must stop. It seems obvious, but many writers would prefer to be in the unending finesse business than in the publication business. In journalism there's a make-your-mind-up time. You learn to recognise that time. When it comes along, you type out a clean draft, invest in an SAE and paperclip (never a staple) hurl it into a letter box and get on with the next one. The stamped self-addressed envelope is the one that will bring your feature back to you if you are not lucky enough to have it published by the first publication you send it to, but if you *are* lucky enough to happen on an editor who sends back material. Not all of them do.

Newspaper editors tend to have a love/hate relationship with freelances. Most editors would be happy to do without them altogether, in the belief that staff people are more controllable and are there in emergencies. On the other hand, there are few editors around who do not have their own pet freelance; some one whose neatly typed envelope brings a promise of clean copy, tailored carefully to the needs of the paper concerned. Unfortunately, not enough freelances provide that kind of service. Wind any editor up on the subject, and he will go on forever about the ill-presented, badly thought-out, appallingly written bits of irrelevant drivel which arrive on his desk every day.

As a result, editors tend to shy away from admitting that they use any freelance work, for fear that the admission will provoke still further influxes of rubbish. One editor with a quarter of a century of experience told me that he constantly finds freelance writers approaching papers in a hamfisted, badly planned way.

"They don't bother to first of all find out the style of the paper," he told me."And far too many writers are far too serious in their writing habits—not enough light reading. A phone call in advance, followed up by copy, and a phone call a few days after copy is sent, will see more freelance work in the paper than in the paper basket."

So the first step to having a piece accepted by any newspaper is to work out what the newspaper is interested in, and in what style the feature should be written. There is no point in sending lengthy upmarket writing to a sex-obsessed tabloid or vice versa, but people do it all the time. I once edited a glossy magazine for teenagers, which was all about fashion and rock music and how to improve (or initiate) your love life. In every mailbag came solemn travel features ('The Rose-Red City, Half as Old as Time') articles on simplifying housework ('Burned on material in a ceramic saucepan may be readily removed using a solution of...') and items on surviving the traumas of advancing years ('Just because your husband has retired doesn't mean you have, too.') What I needed were features on sexually transmitted diseases, quizzes designed to help readers establish their relative levels of sophistication, cool profiles of newcomers to the hit parade or snippets of streetsmarts. When I had the time, and when the writers provided an SAE, I sent them back with a rejection slip and a little note indicating that they would be better advised to try a publication aimed at the age group they were writing for. Not many editors can find the time to be mentors at long distance, but many do. Some material you never get back, even if you have sent an SAE, because the editor you have sent it to is busy or lazy or disorganised. They're human, too, remember? Some material comes back with a blunt, unsigned rejection slip.

Occasionally you'll get a rejection slip on which someone has scribbled a couple of lines. Over 15 years, I have kept all of these. They say things like:

> This is too long for us. See if you can bring it down to about 600 words and let us see it again.

I did, and they used it.

> Your feature is well-written, but we covered this topic too recently to run it again.

The problem with this one was that my SAE was very small, and they had to fold up the feature to get it into the envelope, so that on its return, the text was trisected with paper wrinkles. I ironed it on its reverse side and sent it out again. Two tries later, it was accepted.

> Liked it. Won't use it.

This one maddened me, but I sent it elsewhere by the next mail. The editor I sent it to this time lost it.

> Not suitable. Are you interested in writing health column?

Was I? Would a duck swim? For 5 years, I wrote about health every week. I wrote about dry eyes and wet feet, about tragic deaths and medical breakthroughs, about diets and diuretics. Every feature I wrote sparked off another idea in my mind (see IDEAS, page 56) I developed a filing system replete with medical wisdom, and during each one of the five years I suffered from the medical student's classic problem of believing I was incubating whatever obscure disease I was writing about at any given time.

You need a dollop of positive thinking when a rejection slip arrives. To prevent its arrival, you need sales skills. The more established you are, the easier is the sales cycle on any feature. You know an editor. You ring her. You run through your list of ideas. She gives the nod to three and you get cracking.

But when you are an unknown, making your first approach to a particular newspaper, Ms B Gotten, Editor of the Woman's Page, is unlikely to react favourably to a phone call detailing your new and original idea for a thousand-word article. She has not, remember, seen your work before, and therefore is keeping her wits about her if she declines to buy sight unseen. You must, therefore, write the feature and send it with a happy humble covering letter by way of self-introduction.

When submitting material, at least in the early stages, the alcoholic's system of living a day at a time should apply. An amazing number of people cheerfully approach editors to whom they are unknown, saying: "I have this great idea for a weekly column." Editors back off rapidly, as this approach shows not only a lack of appreciation of the day-to-day space problems of a newspaper, which call for an absolute minimum of rigid blocks of space allocated in advance, but also an incredible bumptiousness. It is much more realistic for newcomers to try to sell once-off pieces.

So, let us assume that you have written an 800 word feature about noise pollution. You have checked that the Weekly Post-Press middle pages usually run articles of about that length. By telephoning the paper, you have got the name of the Features Editor in charge of those middle pages, and you have the spelling right. When writers submitting material to me sent it to Terri Prone I was always put off. It made me wonder about the quality of research that had gone into the piece and speculate about the economics of having every fact and spelling in it checked by somebody else. This is the syndrome which happens on aircraft; if you sit down in a 757 and the reading light will not work, you are immediately given furiously to thinking about the quality of engine maintenance and the morale of the hydraulics. In addition, I felt somewhat squashed. My name is a poor thing but mine own, and editors, just like everybody else, enjoy hearing their names and seeing their names and a mis-spelling is a needless irritant.

Titles matter, too. If someone has moved from being Features Editor to being Sports Editor, then sending your piece about sheet metal sculptures to him will be less than effective. Either it will go to him in the Sports Department, in which case you are unknowingly relying on his willingness to be your mailman and get the thing to the new dame in Features, or it will go to the new dame, who will not be pleased that you have not noted her recent promotion. A quick telephone call will ensure that Mr Colm Inch is still Features editor, or that Ms Ann Thrope has not been moved from the Arts page. That can happen in the time it takes to have a reference book like the *Writers' and Artists' Yearbook* printed and published. Sending things to editors and addressing them as their predecessors does not enhance the chances of your piece succeeding, since the logical inference to be drawn from it is that you do not read their newspaper very closely.

Now you have the name of the man or woman you're going to send it to. We will assume that you have typed out the copy, double spaced on one side of decent sheets of paper. We will assume that all sheets are the same size. That you have provided large margins. From the presentation point of view, it is important to use paper clips instead of staples, to hold the pages of your feature together. It is vital to keep a carbon copy. Newspapers occasionally lose material sent to them, and crying despairingly that it was your only copy will achieve nothing except a conviction in the editor's mind that you are a troublesome dope.

Your covering letter should be no more than two or three sentences long. No editor wants to know the biography of a freelance sending a speculative piece of copy. Just mention any other items you have had published, give a reason for assuming it might suit him, indicate that there is an SAE enclosed, and sign your name.

The piece itself should have a title page on it. That title page should give the name of the piece (although newspapers virtually never use the title the writer chooses for a piece), a description of what it is about, the name and address of the writer and a rough word count. Like this:

A "rough word count" means precisely that. Do not waste your time going through your copy counting words aloud. Count the words in three separate lines and work out the average. Multiply that average by the number of lines in the feature, and that constitutes a rough word count. If you have a word processor, the chances are that it will have a word count capacity, which simplifies your labours.

```
Deafened by Decibels


Noise pollution now a
  major health threat


        650 words



Joe Bloggs
102 New Park, Midtown,
Burgersville 8.
Telephone: 500000
```

The next step is to examine the layout of the first page of actual text. Now that modern technology has taken root in so many newspapers, there is less requirement for rigidly formal presentation, but it is always a good idea to type the first paragraph of your feature all on its own on page one. That page should have, on the left, your name and where you work from and in the top right hand corner, the catchline and folio number. The catchline is simply a key word which indicates to a sub-editor or printer the story each page contains. So this feature about noise will have its pages numbered—Noise 1, Noise 2, Noise 3 etc.

This is how the first page of your feature might look.

In the case of our fictional story about noise levels, the catchline is simple and obvious, but choosing words to use as catchlines can be a quirky business. Even if your story concerns a shoot-out at the local supermarket or a fleet of coffins, never catchline it "Kill" or "Dead." They are both instructions to the printer that the story is not being used and the chances are that a piece so catchlined will end up in the waste-paper basket. Another point to watch is the dirty catchline. It is one of the incontrovertible laws of newspapers that if you catchline your story "Tits" or "Knickers" the word will end up in print, making a nasty comment on your story, and leaving egg in large spoonfuls on your face. Finally, never use a catchline which is obscure. I knew a fashion writer who used to drive subs mad by catching her stories with odd clothing trade terms. The sub-editor would be screaming for her copy, and someone would eventually turn up several sheets marked "Faggoting" and "Jap" to cries of "Well how the hell was I to know that was fashion?"

In any feature, you have to grasp your reader warmly by the throat early on. You are not writing a short story. The person reading your piece may be on a bus, fighting for elbow space and distracted by the vehicle's stops and starts. Or the reader may be in a hurry, quickly selecting what justifies the expenditure of time and what does not. There are always other attractions inside the newspaper that prints your feature. And outside it; think of the number of readers who, although they have a newspaper on their lap, have a television on in the same room and another person to talk to. All of these competing

---

Bloggs/Midtown   **Noise 1**

```
Daily life is deafening millions,
according to experts at the
Glungschberg Environment Institute.
Noise levels have soared in the
past twenty years, because of
modern technology in the workplace,
more machinery in the home, and
greatly increased traffic in our
streets. The end result is that
people are going deaf in larger
numbers earlier in life, and that
more of us are coming under
physical and psychological
pressure because of the assault
on our eardrums.
```

M/F

---

interests mean that you must get as many of the essentials as possible into the early paragraphs. Editors hate stories where the vital questions Who? What? Where? How? are not answered by three. This is for several reasons. Journalism is all about story-telling, and good journalistic storytelling does not leave the reader wondering for long about who the main characters are and what the subject is. Journalistic storytelling is based on the assumption that people have other things to do with their time, and so it's vital to get to the point quickly, before one of those rival possibilities becomes more attractive.

Sub-editors hate features which are slow to start because they know it may be necessary to cut the story at the last moment, and a wandering waffle is very difficult to cut.

Two hints in this area.

1 Some writers find it difficult to start in first gear. They need to rev on the spot for a while before they get moving. If you're that kind of writer, what you must do is get the feature written, and then read it through, asking yourself "At what point do I stop revving and get moving?" It may be that this happens after one paragraph. It may take three. But the difference is palpable. Once you have identified that point, cut everything that came before it.

2 Somerset Maugham said that writers should re-read their material, find the three things they like best, and cut them out as likely to be self-indulgent, non-functional and merely decorative.

All of what we have covered thus far in this chapter is geared to help you create and place material in features pages. This is not to say that newspapers will not accept news stories from freelances. They will. But regular contributions in the news area are usually confined to NUJ members. (See Chapter 12). Even if you live in an area where major newspapers are not directly represented, you will find that national newspapers often have a casual relationship with a particular journalist called a "stringer," who passes on worthwhile stories to the paper from his area. Stringers sometimes operate on the basis of lineage—that is the fee paid per line of story accepted by the paper. Some stringers also have a retainer fee from a particular paper. (Retainers, where they exist, are rarely large. They seem to be used more as a means of recognising the relationship between the paper and the journalist than as a serious contribution to his/her finances.)

In addition, relatively few new stories just happen when a writer is passing by. I was in a street once where a man threatened to throw himself off a roof, I was in a taxi passing the Old Bailey when someone blew a bit of it up, and I was in Nassau Street, Dublin parking my car when a bomb went off as part of what became known as Bloody Friday. Three news stories I just happened on in fifteen years of writing—and even that would be regarded as exceptional. Your chances of getting into the features pages are immeasurably better, although once a newspaper knows you and once you are a member of the appropriate trade union, it is possible that they will use you as a freelance news reporter, sending you out to write about protests, disasters or Government meetings. The main difference between the news and the features section of a newspaper is that in features you have more room to be good or bad, and a little more freedom of style. Freedom of style is important, because a great deal of what goes into features material has not got the inbuilt saleability of news. It is based on happenings which occur every year (the Paris collections, trends in summer holidays, what the Budget means to YOU...) and without an inventive touch, the material can end up deader than cold baked beans.

Two examples, here, of where style rescued otherwise routine stories from boredom. One was a fairly routine complaining feature about income tax. The writer turned the thing on its head and talked ambiguously all the way through about —x appeal, who had it and who hadn't it. The general effect was funny and risque, and the essential points were made in a lively way. Only in the final line did it emerge that the missing letters made up the word TAX. The other piece was an interview with a writer of bubbling below-stairs-type reminiscences who had been interviewed by every newspaper and radio programme this side of the Sudan in the preceding two years. The writer put the piece together as a little playlet, including stage directions. This clever device not only made the piece more readable, but also enabled the writer to point out that the author laughed incessantly without being insulting about it. After each of the author's comments appeared, in brackets, the stage direction (LAUGHS).

The point is not that gimmicky presentation of a piece is the way to an editor's heart, but that every writer should strive

- to say something new, or
- to say something old in a new way.

It sounds simple, but dozens of manuscripts arrive at newspaper offices every day in which solid, worthy, predictable and old points are made in solid, worthy, old and predictable ways. Newspapers want new things. If you cannot deliver a new thing, you must package an old thing so that it becomes interesting all over again. Do it well enough and you will discover that many publications that claim that they use little or no freelance material are more open in practice than in policy statement. Several years ago, as an experiment, I talked to five publications that gave me clear indication that they were not interested in freelance contributions. I then sent each of them a feature under a pseudonym. Four of them were accepted. It was a lucky week, but the fact is that quite often, newspapers and magazines that publicly adopt a negative posture in order to protect themselves from an avalanche of poor quality freelance material are unembarrassed by the desire to deviate from that stance when they are intrigued by well-targeted material.

Once your piece has been accepted, it is in the hands of sub-editors. They like clean copy with big margins and nice gaps between the paragraphs for them to make notes in, and that is why you will find this advice appearing *ad nauseam*. Sub-editors also can enhance your piece by skilful editing. Occasionally, one of them slips a cog and alters the text so that, in print, it makes precious little sense to you. Squabbling about who edited what in your piece is a mistake. Subs are working under pressure, they've subbed bigger and better than you and they have long memories.

An example of insensitive subbing which is nobody's fault is where the end of a piece is chopped off, leaving an article "up in the air." This usually happens when an urgent piece comes in too late for space to be made by delicate editing of an existing piece, so someone picks a likely spot and chops the tail off. Complaining about it is like sniping at a fireman for dirtying your doorstep when he came to rescue you from your burning house. Complaints will certainly be seen in that light by the sub involved.

Humility is a great help when submitting material to newspapers. A brief note, enclosed with your piece and your stamped self-addressed envelope, saying that you'd be glad, in the event of a rejection, to know roughly what was wrong with the piece, can be both helpful to you, if they take you up on it, and flattering to them. On the other hand, ringing up to crib about the smallness of your by-line, the inconspicuous situation your feature found itself in, or the misprints in it will get you nowhere fast.

One of the worries that freelances have is that in submitting their material they are laying themselves open to abuse. They fear, in other words, that someone will read their piece about the beauty of red diesel tractors, bung it back to them with a note saying "unsuitable" and then sit down to write a feature using all their good material. This has never happened to me, but I am aware of occasional rumblings from freelances who feel it an ever-present danger. Some of them send up flags about their worry by either typing a legend or using a rubber stamp to imprint one on the title page of their piece, indicating that first rights in Britain or Europe or the Isle of Wight ONLY are offered, that if anybody wants to publish one sentence of this feature anywhere else, they must send a delegation first to the United Nations, and if these conditions of offer are broken in any way, the wicked editor breaking them will be sent to the

Tower of London and polished once a day with a Brillo Pad.

These formal threats on the front of features are, in my view, pointless irritants that do not achieve the objective their users hope for—a respectful view of the writer as a solid professional whose work must not be tampered with. Instead, they tend to create a perception of the writer as a paranoid amateur who greatly over-estimates the value of his personal contribution to the world of print.

The *Writer's and Artist's Yearbook* will give you all of the technical details you need about copyright. In general, though, what you need to do is keep a copy of whatever you submit, notify the NUJ if your stuff appears re-written under someone else's name, write a stiff note to the editor involved, and do not send them any more. Before you take action, however, reflect that there is no copyright on ideas. Only the words you put together and the material unique to you is copyright. Any other fool in the world can decide to write about tractors, and if he happens to cover the same ground, and if that ground is easily discoverable by anybody with an encyclopedia and an uncle in farming, then you really have no beef. It works both ways too. Reading someone else's article may spark off a piece on the same theme in your mind, and that's fair enough. Nick any of their piece directly and you are in trouble, and rightly so. Never, by the way, think that because the article appeared in a pre-war Reader's Digest the writer is dead and forgotten about. The long arm of coincidence is what has choked many a happy plagiarist in the past: witness the American presidential candidate who in 1987 used second-hand and unattributed speech material in public and was nailed for it.

A trainee of mine once got blind with rage when a magazine sent back a feature she had written, saying it was unsuitable, only to publish a feature covering precisely the same ground with rather less style than she had provided, about two weeks later. The problem here was lead time. The feature was about choosing Christmas toys for toddlers. She submitted it to the magazine on the 23rd of November. The issue of the magazine carrying a similar feature appeared on the 3rd of December.

It all added up to a scenario of theft and pillage as far as the rejected writer was concerned, and she was for taking the magazine to the Supreme Court immediately if not sooner. A little investigation knocked the struts out from under this particular scenario. The lead time of this magazine was eight weeks. In other words, from the time the editorial material was accepted, agreed, marked up and sent to the printer to the time the magazine actually appeared was eight weeks. So the issue of the 3rd of December had "gone to bed" early in October. By the time my trainee submitted her feature, it was unsuitable because the right time had passed and the need had been met by someone else.

Lead times matter. Always check that your feature, if it is topical, will be in the newspaper or magazine office before the deadline. Lead times and the deadlines they demand vary tremendously. A good rule of thumb is that the glossier the magazine, the longer the lead time. One specialist publication for which I have written and provided colour photographs came out fourteen months after you delivered a commissioned piece. By the time your feature was in print, you had forgotten about it, aged considerably or even changed career. Even within newspapers, there are different lead times for different pages. News stories, if they are important, will be taken almost up to the moment the paper goes to press. Feature material, on the other hand, needs to arrive much sooner. On national papers, the feature pages tend to be in preparation two or three days before the day of publication, so a feature designed for those pages will be too late if it arrives the day before publication. Smaller local papers and freesheets vary in their deadlines. A quick phone call to the newspaper office will sort out when it should be on the editor's desk. The great trick is to hit that magic moment when one paper has just gone out, and the editor is beginning to think about the next one. With practice, this is easy to achieve.

Although most newspapers and magazines take up a virtuous stance which implies that their advertising people never even *meet* their writing people, because they do not want their priorities dented or their writers tainted, the fact is that when a newspaper or magazine is just about to go to bed, and a full page advertisement comes in, the writers go into second place, the copy which has been set in type gets tossed out, and in goes the ad. Unfortunately, a curious spin-off of this is what happens to the features on the page that was removed. They were good features. But they got pulled. Three or four days later, because they have been sitting around, they have become de-valued in the eyes of the sub-editors and are quite likely to be permanently spiked. If that happens, the newspaper may, if it has told you it's going to use your piece, pay you either in full or offer a cancellation fee, and you are free to sell it to some other publication, assuming that it has not, in the interim, lost topicality.

The amount you can expect for a feature published in a newspaper or magazine varies wildly. Some smaller newspapers and freesheets pay nothing to freelances, even though they will print material sent to them, operating on the principle that the world is full of amateur writers whose personal need for reassurance is such that appearing in print is much more important to them than being paid anything. There is just sufficient truth in this self-serving belief to ensure that non-paying publications have a considerable body of copy made available to them by eager would-be writers.

Then there are larger newspapers which operate a variant on the same theme. These papers have pages or areas within their publication devoted to unsolicited features which follow lines like "I Feel Passionately About..." or "There Should be a Law to Prevent..." With or without talent, virtually everybody can produce one or two of those kind of features every year. So there's a constant supply from people who are quite surprised to be paid as well as published. Regular journalists, whether staff or freelance, hate these pages and the people who write for them. Cheap labour, they say bitterly.

Apart from the publications which use material without paying for it or without paying much for it, there is still enormous variation in the size of the cheque you can expect from different publications. What one paper will pay £25 for, another will value at £53. In the beginning, the priority is to be published, to build up a portfolio. Once that is done, the writer who wants to make a living by his/her pen or typewriter begins to keep records and assess which are the markets that make most financial sense. By way of counterpoint to this commercially good advice, I must admit that I have written, year after year, for publications that paid me buttons, simply because I liked the publication or got along well with the commissioning editor. Woman does not live by bread alone.

It helps if you put a value on your time. It came as a great blow to me, a few years ago, when I was running a business, to discover that one of the most time-consuming contracts we actively sought each year was not worth a damn to our figures. So said our accountant. But, we said, the budgets are huge. Yes, said the accountant. And so are the expenses. But, we said, look at what they pay us. Yes, said the accountant. Throughput, not profit. But, we said, would we be better to stop doing this thing and do something quite different? The accountant nodded wisely. It was only later that I applied this grim suggestion to some of my journalistic work, and realised that some jobs I had undertaken regularly had entailed an enormous expenditure in shoe leather, petrol and time, and that I might have been better off sitting at home in bed planning a feature which would bring me more personal profit. Writers need to have a value on their time, so that they choose on the basis of what will give them a living, and devote a commercially acceptable amount of time to each commission.

One freelance writer of my acquaintance does precisely that. When I was editing a woman's magazine at one point, I rang him with a problem.

"Herbie," I said. "I need a six part series. Historical romance. Set in Regency times. But I only have £160."

He never missed a beat.

"Well, Terry," he said. "I can certainly supply you with £160-worth of historical romance."

The message was clear. Literature I was not going to get.

Extensive research to ensure that the piece was peppered with contemporary slang I was not going to get. I was going to get a lively competent job done in the amount of time justified by the fee of £160. The end result was most satisfactory to both sides.

There is no doubt that any reasonably intelligent and disciplined freelance can make a respectable wage from writing. A few years after the first edition of this book came out, I was contacted by someone who had bought a copy. When she came to see me, she showed it to me. It was like an old cookbook. The spine had been broken by vigorous use, half the pages were turned down at the corners for easy reference, and there were scribbles all over the margins. It was a workbook. That had happened because the owner had been given it as a present when she had been stricken by one of those recurring diseases which lays you on your back in a hospital or home bed for six months at a time. When it first struck, her husband had just been made redundant, and things were looking extremely grim. A friend gave her my book with the cheering suggestion that since they were now poverty stricken and since there was little the disabled woman could do from bed other than write, she had better learn how. A year later she was the main earner in the family, and has never looked back.

A living can certainly be made, although it often takes quite a long time to build up contacts with editors and to develop a work-schedule which provides enough money regularly. But the sooner you start submitting material, the sooner you can find out if you will make enough to support yourself.

Fear that you might not make sufficient to live on should never hinder you from making the first moves towards writing. What have you to lose? Even if you decide against throwing your bread on the freelance waters, you can still write as a side-line.

Freelance writing is great fun. It is also exhausting, worrying and inconsistent in its returns. The person who coined the phrase "feast or famine" has to have been a freelance writer, because we freelances are always either biting our nails down to the elbow for lack of work, or sleeping three hours a night because so much has suddenly been offered.

Freelance means a host of different things. It covers the man who thinks it a bad year when his earnings don't cover two continental holidays and a change of car, who never tackles a story unless he is sure of selling it to two Irish markets and a US buyer. And it covers the mother-of-three who provides a much needed supplement to the family income, or financial independence for herself, by knocking out several feature stories a week when her children are at school.

Your chance of getting there, and hanging in there as a freelance, are improved if you obey some of the unwritten rules:

DOS

- *Do* treat editors and their publications with respect. Learn about them. About the lengths and styles they prefer. About their names and titles

- *Do* get the presentation of your material right.

- *Do* learn from rejection slips.

- *Do* put a value on your time.

- *Do* read your material, catch typos and remove redundancies before you submit it.

DON'TS

- *Don't* complain about the way they edit your stuff or about the way they laid it out on the page, or the way they lost it or the money they paid you or the manner of rejection.

- *Don't* be afraid to check with a magazine or newspaper about names, titles or lead times.

- *Don't* start where you are. Start where the listener is.

- *Don't* try journalism if you secretly feel it's beneath you.

- *Don't* cause editors problems by forgetting to give them names, addresses, telephone numbers and word counts.

Chapter 4

Ideas, Interviews and Personality Profiles

I improve on misquotation.

Cary Grant

- I'd love to be a freelance journalist, but where do you get the ideas?

- The prospect of interviewing somebody famous terrifies me.

- What makes a good personality profile?

There were two of them. One was the cub reporter. The other was the editor. The cub reporter was terrified, in a pervasive unfocussed way. The editor was directive but kindly. He praised her good work and explained to her how she had made the mistakes she did make. But the anxiety level seemed to stay constant. He couldn't figure it. Eventually, he decided to ask her about it.

"I just have this nightmare that one of these days I'm going to be trying to write stories for you and there's going to be nothing there," she said desperately.

"You mean you'll get writer's block?"

"No. I mean that there won't be anything to write about. Nothing will have happened. Nothing in the whole previous twenty-four hours."

The editor was silent. A slow smile washed over him and his hands came up to sketch out the headline in the air.

T016461

"Jesus," he said. "Can you imagine it? TODAY THERE IS NO NEWS! Nobody ever had THAT before."

Too many would-be writers are like the cub reporter— anxious about a potential lack of stories, and unlike that editor who was willing to make a story out of anything.

Anybody who asks more than once "where would I get the ideas from?" should go into another business, because it's a disqualifying query on a par with some, aspiring ballet dancer, asking "where would I get the feet from?" Feet and ideas are generally there, like Everest. It is a matter of noticing them and making the most of them.

Noticing them is the first problem. Last year, when I was training a group of people in a business to produce a staff newsletter, the ideas-generation problem surfaced, and I was startled by a suggestion from one of the participants that a £10 prize be awarded for the group member who, the following day, produced a list of topics for features based on a walk around his own quite small office building. The winner came up with:

- **Phone Fear**
  One of the executives had a hangup about using the phone, getting his secretary to make and receive the vast majority of his calls. Cornered, he admitted that when the phone rang, it filled him with dread. Topic for the feature: is there phone phobia?

- **Sick Furnishings**
  If you're an asthmatic, should you work in a room with curtains and carpets? If you have contact lenses, should you work with a VDU? Why do so many people suffer back problems—poorly designed chairs?

- **Doodles**
  In off moments, people doodle. What? And why? Any difference between male and female doodles? Any significance to particular kinds of doodle?

- **The After Lunch Syndrome**
  Some people come back to work after lunch half asleep. Is it

because of what they eat or the very fact that they eat? Are there "sleepy foods"?

- **Fax Mania**
  FAX caught on largely by word of mouth. Now, FAX machines are spewing out mountains of paper and are being used for unsolicited marketing material. Where will it end?

- **Memo - itis**
  Why do some companies have a memo culture, when, in other companies, staff talk to each other?

- **White collar wastage**
  What do white collar workers steal from the workplace? Any trends? How many get caught?

- **Secrets**
  Every computer has a device whereby you can put code words on information you don't want other people to access. How do people think up code words? How do people dream up the secret numbers for their briefcase locks? How do they remember the secret numbers that make their credit cards work?

- **Creches**
  Do creches at the workplace actually function, or is it too distracting for mothers/fathers to have their kids so close to them?

- **Nicknames**
  Why are some bosses called The Chief, some known as God, and some entitled Attila the Hun? Do people know about their nicknames?

- **Painkiller Addiction**
  Is it possible to become addicted to ordinary everyday painkillers? (One staff member had been observed to take painkillers virtually every day.)

- **Time Management**
  Do those little leather pouch diaries work, or do their owners

just have a better structured method of wasting time?

- **Outlaw Coffee Breaks**
  Is the formal coffee break a waste of time? Would people be more productive if they simply left their desks, made coffee and brought it back as they wanted.

- **More Flexi**
  Why is flex-time so limited? Why can't workers come in at six in the morning, work to six in the evening, and take a fortnight off every now and again?

- **Response Rules OK**
  How quickly should phones be answered? Should people ever be left on "hold"? Is music when you're on hold a good idea or would a news bulletin be more interesting?

- **Slang**
  'Nuff said, OK? I mean, you and me's cool, so this one would be the business.

- **Paper Pollution**
  Every office churns out tons of waste paper each year. Yet few arrange to have it re-cycled. Implications for trees, pollution and cost.

- **Lease versus Buy**
  If a staff member is to get a new car, which makes more income tax sense— to lease it or buy it?

- **Alcoholism and Privacy**
  If you're an alcoholic joining a new firm, should you tell them that you suffer from the illness if you're not currently drinking? Do your co-workers have any right to know?

- **Cheap Chemical Highs**
  One company is rumoured to have called in health professionals to deal with a problem arising because of quite casual Tipp-Ex and glue sniffing on the part of their typing pool.

- **Office Romance — Illicit**
  Why does it happen? Who gains? Who loses? The "other woman" role.

- **Habits**
  Some people drum their fingers, some ruffle the pages of books they're reading, some whistle through their teeth. Why? And which is most annoying.

- **Desk Decorations**
  Why do some people have pictures of their wives and kids on their desk? Why do some people have jokey statuettes?

- **Inhuman voices**
  Is there a real live person behind the telephone Speaking Clock?

- **Hello in Confidence**
  If a company has an executive on the road with a car phone or a cellular phone, should he or she talk in code because of electronic eavesdropping? How can you find out who might be eavesdropping?

- **Illiteracy/innumeracy**
  How people who can't do sums survive. How people who can't read pretend.

- **Lost Baggage**
  Why do some executives always find themselves in Amsterdam when their luggage is in Bahrain?

- **Lunchtime Cards**
  Card playing is one lunchtime option. Squash is another. Running is a third. Is actual lunch becoming less important?

- **Stinks**
  If someone reeks of garlic, should they be allowed to get away with it in a crowded office. How do you tell someone they have BO or halitosis?

- **News Freaks**
  Some people can't focus on the day unless they get regular

doses of news. Why? What does it matter to your job that someone is having trouble in Outer Mongolia?

- **Cleaning Ladies**
  Why are they mostly women? What are people's pet peeves in regard to the tidying of their office after hours? What are they paid?

- **Frequent Flyer**
  Increasingly, airlines have Frequent Flyer programmes. How do you find out, if your company needs to fly you around a lot, what's the best airline in terms of getting a free flight to somewhere pleasant at the end of a working year?

- **Corporate Culture**
  Is it just a buzz word?

- **Sales Reps**
  Their habits (hanging up their jackets in the car when they drive, calling you by your first name, giving you an extra warm handshake.) Why you agree to see them. When you buy from them.

- **The Saturday Spend**
  The younger people in the office tended to head off on a Saturday morning to spend a good deal of the money they had earned during the week. Why? On what?

- **Women on the Promotion Ladder**
  Few women making it to the top. Prejudice or female lack of ambition?

- **Spot the Perfume**
  One of the fellows in the office had once worked for a cosmetic company. It had left him with an ability to spot precisely what perfume a woman would wear—even if she had no perfume on that particular day. Typecasting? Stereotyping? Or good observation? Didn't matter—he was still able to tell if you were an Arpege type or a Chanel Number 5 type.

• Car Accidents

One staff member had recently been in a car smash. In the Emergency room of the hospital, a doctor had casually said, examining him, "I suppose you were driving a Volkswagen." Puzzled by the accuracy of the guess, the victim asked more, and found that the hospital staff had worked out that particular injuries to particular parts of the body were associated with particular car models. (They also said, for what it's worth, that if you happened to be in a Volvo in a collision, you were likely to be brought into hospital suffering only from shock...).

Almost forty ideas were pulled together overnight by a non-journalist gazing into space and trying to figure what was interesting about the place she worked in and the people she worked with. Not all of them were great ideas, but every one of them was worth trying.

Getting ideas is a habit of mind. You look at everything you encounter in a day as a potential feature, you tease out how you might make it interesting, and you make notes of the process. As editor of a magazine, I remember a feature submitted to me which dealt with what people do at traffic lights. People in cars. The writer had noticed that some people gaze into space, some people watch passersby, some people make car telephone calls, some people paint their nails. She interviewed dozens at a traffic lights in the middle of the city. The oddball element she discovered was an eminent psychiatrist who plays his flute at traffic lights as a way of pre-empting tension. It made for a lovely piece and sparked off a series of "D'you know what *I* do at traffic lights?" contributions to a local radio programme, not all of which were usable. That particular writer was not sitting around hoping that a passing idea might strike her. She was on the trawl.

If you are constantly on an ideas trawl, you find that there are more possible features out there than you could ever write. You get ideas from keeping your eyes open. You get ideas from listening. You get ideas from books you read, programmes you listen to. You get ideas from personal triumphs and disasters. But you must make notes. At all times. In all places. The most frustrating thing in the world is to have had an idea and to be unable to retrieve it after a distraction has intervened between you and it. Ideas, unfortunately, do not wait until you are in situ at your desk, ready and waiting for them. They happen along when you are in thirty six inches of bathwater, when you are behind the wheel of a car, halfway through nappying a baby, or on the turn in the bed at night. Tell yourself "It's OK, this is such a good idea, I'll remember it" and I can guarantee you will not.

Get to a note pad quickly and write it down. One of the great boons to writers is the Post-it note. These are the little yellow pads of pull-off note pages with a bit of adhesive at the top, so you can stick the sheet to a telephone or a diary or a worksurface and later detach it without having done any damage to the recipient area. I have Post-it notes stuck all over my life. They're on walls everywhere. Just in case an idea strikes. There is always a big one stuck at the front of any book I'm reading, so I do not have to go away and search if the book sets me off on a train of thought or provides a quotation worth remembering. A slightly smaller one sticks to the flat middle bit of the steering wheel in my car, so that ideas surfacing *en route* can be noted in traffic jams. In addition, I have a natty little gadget donated by my husband, which sits beside our bed. It's a little pad with a pen at the top. When you lift the pen up, a tiny light comes on to illuminate the pad, so that when you wake in the middle of the night, you can quickly note that brilliant idea without disturbing the entire neighbourhood—or worse still, postpone writing it down for FEAR that you MIGHT disturb the neighbourhood.

Every feature you write should create spin-off ideas. For example, a magazine commissioned a feature from me about back pain. I wrote it. In the course of writing it, I came upon individual sufferers who swore by chiropractors—and medical experts who were surprisingly positive about same. Out of that came a three part series on the Bone Bashers for a daily newspaper. In the course of doing the research for that series, someone said that back pain sufferers tended to be workaholics.

A little note of this was stuck in a file, and later, short of an idea, I came upon it and got launched on a search for household name workaholics. That feature complete, I noted that one of the household name workaholics swore by his goldfish bowl as a tension-reducer. His theory was that anybody who looked for a half an hour at goldfish experienced a cosmic calm. Several months later, this became the basis for a feature on natural tranquillisers. This in turn, led to a feature about how to get the best out of the pills you take, which covered when to take them, how to take them (standing up, would you believe, and with a glass of water) and where to store them.

It goes on and on. Ideas for features can be generated in an infinite cycle. That's the positive side to the story. The less positive side is that, if you are constantly on the lookout, always making notes, carefully filing those notes, you can sometimes feel as if you work forty-eight hours a day.

Filing features you have submitted is amazingly helpful. Buy yourself a second-hand filing cabinet. They're dirt cheap. Keep a copy of everything that is submitted, with the date of submission on it. File according to subject: Profiles, Health Features, Funnies, Children, etc. Where a feature gets published, pin the published version to the draft, so that you have a record of what was actually used. The latter can be helpful when you want to use some of the material again in a different area, because it can establish for you precisely what the newspaper cut and what it did not cut. Once it has been printed, you cannot use it again. But you may find that a couple of paragraphs, cut by one newspaper for reasons of space, can go into a feature for another newspaper.

Simply going through old files, when you're going through an ideas famine, is likely to give you new energy and a line-up of under-exploited topics.

Generating and managing ideas is a crucial skill for a freelance. So is research.

If you write about the funny things your children say, or your experience on the 44A bus, then you do not need to do research. If you write about people or issues or facts or figures or trends, then you do need to do research. Or, more simply, to get information. To a new writer, it can be a curiously daunting task. Where to start?

Let's pick a simple idea. You want to write about St Valentine's Day. The first thing is to make a list of what you want to know. Like this:

- St Valentine. Who? When? How associated with love? Real or legendary?

- Big business? Cards? Flowers? Gifts? Kiss-a-Grams?

- Commercial? Crude?

The first series of questions should take you to an Encyclopedia. Other books, like Charles Panati's *Extraordinary Origins of Everyday Things* (Harper and Row, 1987) can give you more useful detail. Your local library has encyclopedias and, even better, often has the other books referred to at the end of the paragraph in the encyclopedia. Throw yourself on the mercy of the librarian. Some will look at you blankly and indicate that it is your job to find whatever you are looking for. Some will be knowledgable and helpful and, over a period of time, will become your ally in seeking for information.

After the encyclopedia, in this instance, comes the Tame Expert. The reference book establishes that St Valentine was a bishop, whose martyrdom was used by the Church as a means of deflecting interest from the old pagan feast of Lupercal onto a more acceptable semi-religious celebration of human love. If you can find a clergyman who is also an historian or who is interested in myth and legend, then you may get some useful pointers, or, better still, quotes from him. Ask some priest you know for help. People asked for help are astonishingly eager to give it, especially if the help asked is unexpected. Once you have reached a Church historian who is a good talker, pick his brains at great length, and, when you go home afterwards, do two things:

1 Write him a letter saying "thank you".

2 Record his name, title, address and telephone number in your address book.

Both of these mean that when you need to contact the man again, whether it is in three months time or in three years time, you can reach him and he has some chance of remembering, positively, who you are. As part of your investment in your career, buy a big solid address book into which every name and phone number of every contact you ever make will go, plus a note of what they talked about. Make sure that the address book has enough pages to cope with several years of contacts, and enough space on each page to accommodate snippets of information on each contact. Opening my own at random, I find a name on one page, and a note, in brackets, saying "Good talkative chemist with a bee in his bonnet about ecology," while another page credits a women as being "middle aged mum with strong ideas on working students." I may never again need to do a feature on working students or ecology, but if I do, the names are there. Furthermore, if some friend in the same business comes to me asking for some contact, I can do a swap, just as I beg names from a man I know who's an expert on the pop business. Your contacts book is the most vital single piece of equipment you can own, apart from your typewriter.

Your contacts book is your lifeline. It should be filled, after a few years, with telephone numbers nobody will ever find in the telephone book. Be careful where you leave it. Don't lend it. And if you use it in the office, keep a back up copy of it in a chest of drawers at home. Just in case of theft or arson.

All right. Now you have some basic information about St Valentine, and a modern gloss on his importance from your clergyman. Your research is well under way. The next thing is to examine the commercial aspect of the day. Go to your local card shop and make notes of the names of card publishers. Then check those names in the telephone book, and ring them. If you're lucky, you will be put through to an Information Officer or someone who knows all about the Valentine Card business and who will be happy to answer all of your questions about volumes of sales, size of preferred cards, cost of same, number sold throughout the country or the world and global spend on this day. It may be that some of the questions cannot be answered immediately. Ask the informant if they would mind finding out the information and you will come back to them.

Indicate precisely when you will come back, and telephone them at the time you promised. It is usually in his or her interests to be mentioned in a feature, so they will be helpful. If you find that there is nobody at the office which you rang who can be genuinely informative, ask the top person there to steer you towards someone in their international office who can give you the data you need. Don't take "I don't really know" for an answer. Ask for help and keep asking for it.

A department store PRO will gladly fill you in on what kind of gifts are sold for Valentine's. Again, get their name and number. You may later want to do a feature about shoplifting, remember? Your local flower shop may be able to give you information and stories about who buys what and at what cost. Try to get to them at a time when they're not very busy— perhaps when they have just returned from the flower market in the early morning and are having their cup of coffee before starting the day's work—and get them to enlarge on their business.

If you are a warm, curious, appreciative audience (see the section later in this chapter on INTERVIEWING) they will remember details and anecdotes which can be very useful to you.

Finally, you need to browse in shops and talk to people who are buying cards. Find the rudest card you can and the prettiest. Pick the shop assistant's brain as to who is likely to buy the former, who certain to buy the latter. Make notes where you can. Where it would put someone off to feel they were being researched, listen closely and make notes as soon as you get out of the shop.

That's the basics of research. Asking questions. Looking up things. Asking for help.

When you are doing more serious features, you may need to

do double-check research. This is particularly so when you write features which come to the fringe of medicine. If, for example, you discover a fascinating oddball medical man who specialises in allergies, the temptation is to take down everything he says and print it. You cannot do that. You must double check every claim with someone representing the medical establishment before you publish. Even if you decide not to use what the establishment tells you, it is essential that you know the context into which your story fits, and that you have the criteria to judge its value.

Where possible, do your research in person or on the telephone. Writing to people asking them to provide you with information on the following six points is a formal option which rarely pays off. The recipient either say "hell with that" and throws it out, or says "must do that" and puts it on a shelf. If, on the other hand, you turn up on someone's doorstep, it is relatively simple to give you the information and get you moving. If you telephone someone and have your questions planned, you can get a feature's worth of information in ten minutes.

When you are researching something and you run into a stone wall, there are three possibilities:

- They're too busy
- They don't know
- They're hiding something

The first two just call for gentle but relentless persistence on your part. The last should give you encouragement. When someone is hiding something, the something they are hiding will usually make a good story for an enterprising journalist. Do not accuse them of anything. Just keep at them and at everybody else you think might know anything.

When it comes to actually sitting down with an informant and getting a great deal of quotable information from him or her, then we are talking, not just about research skills, but about interviewing skills. Interviewing starts with the "six honest serving men" of Kipling's rhyme:

> I keep six honest serving-men
> (They taught me all I know).
> Their names are What and Why and When,
> And Which and Where and How
>
> I send them over land and sea
> I send them East and West
> But after they have worked for me
> I give them all a rest...

Those six honest serving men are all you need when you are setting out to do an interview. Many novice journalists believe that if they do not have information-laden, deadly impressive questions, they will lose out. Not so. After an interview, what you want, as a writer, are good quotations from the *interviewee*, not a warm recollection of how wise and witty you were. Never concentrate on show-off questions. Instead, listen to the first answer, and out of that answer, frame the next question, which may simply be

> "Why do you say that?"

or

> "When did that happen?"

or

> "Where did you go from there?"

A great question is one which gets the interviewee to be especially revealing; not one which sounds good of itself.

Learn to frame open questions. Never make a big long statement and then invite a "yes" or "no" answer. One quite experienced journalist friend of mine has never learned this, and when interviewing a person at the centre of a controversy, she will say:

> It has been said that your company has shown some disregard
> for the rule of law in relation to its purchases of raw materials
> over the past few years. It is also clear that your company has
> ignored many local by-laws in the disposal of effluent and that

the long term implications of this are very serious. Are you satisfied with your company record?

The interviewee, in this instance, has had several years in which to formulate a response, which, inevitably, starts with an assertion that his company is totally happy with its track record and is regarded internationally as one of the finest companies of its kind, blah, blah, blah.

Short, simple questions are better. Short simple questions based on committed listening. If you listen closely, you will hear more than the words. You will become aware of half-truths, which allow you to push for the full story. You will become aware of inconsistencies, which can be juxtaposed to make a point. You will become aware of possibilities you did not know about before you started the interview. Therefore, you cannot afford to be reading lists of questions or background information; when you are interviewing, you must LOOK and LISTEN. To free yourself to do that, you need to prepare adequately.

In advance of an interview, you should always work out a series of areas through which you want to take the interviewee. NOT a series of *questions*. Just *areas*.

Your notes should be brief, in big print, so you can refer to them quickly and without destroying the relationship you are building up with the person you are interviewing. Use black felt tip pen, print them clearly and use only key words. Concentrate on what you want him/her to *say*, not on what you want to ask.

If you bring cuttings or other reference material to the interview by way of backup, make sure that you have used a highlighter pen to enable you to locate the important bits easily when you are doing the interview. There is nothing more irritating to a VIP who knows he/she's a VIP than to be held while you grope your way through six sheets of photocopied cuttings for some vague reference you just know is going to be important if you can find it.

If you are going to interview an author, with luck you will have a copy of their new book to hand in advance. Read it if you have the time. If you do not have the time to read the book, these are the priority areas: cover blurb, introduction and index. The Index will spark off a famous name or an issue—read the relevant bit and you'll undoubtedly get a question out of it. Use your telephone reference book to reach contacts who might suggest interesting lines of questioning. (When I was 17, in one week, I was sent to interview Laurence Durrell and George Best. Young and pig-ignorant, I knew nothing about either. At notice of a half an hour, there was no way that I could become knowledgable about them. However, some fast brain-picking gave me a sense of direction, an idea of what people who knew them wanted answered by them, and a couple of key references.)

Before you go to the location where the encounter is to happen, put the interviewee's name, title and organisation down on paper in front of you—blanks happen.

Preparation also involves a decision about how you will take notes. If you have shorthand, then you are in the best possible position, because you can stay in eye contact with the person you are talking with while not losing the detail of what they are saying. A tape recorder, properly used, can be a great asset, but only if it is treated as an important tool of your trade. That means putting new batteries into each before every interview, making sure you have enough blank tapes with you, double checking that it is working and, if appropriate, having it serviced regularly.

Picking the best tape-recorder is a complex task. It can be a quite cheap portable cassette machine with an in-built microphone. A separate microphone on the end of a long flex, especially if it sits up on one of those pyramid-shaped stands, can be very distracting for your interviewee, because it so visibly announces that you are recording the conversation. Many interviewees are self-conscious, and if you are asking them questions in a public place like a hotel coffee shop, the idea that other people can see them being interviewed may induce a case of nerves.

Dictaphone tapes can be a good idea if you have a playback

unit. They can be played back at half the speed, which means that a touch-typist can produce a transcript of the interview in no time at all. At the other end of the continuum is a pet machine of mine, produced by FE Electric in the US and available from Hammacher Schlemmer in New York city by mail. This machine is a small solid hand-held job. What makes it special is that, based on technology developed for talking books used by blind people, it can be played back at twice the normal speed without the usual resulting speech distortion. You can understand what is being said at any stage, which can be useful if you are not producing a complete transcript, merely looking for a specific quotable quote.

A machine which gives off a little tweeting noise when it reaches the end of a cassette can help prevent a pitfall I have fallen into a couple of times. This is where you are interviewing somebody, and they become so enthralling that you forget to check if you have reached the end of that side of the tape. By the time you remember, twenty minutes of valuable material has been lost. Preventing this disaster is also helped if you use the longest tapes you can get. This latter suggestion does not work if you are, for example, hoping to place the tape on a local radio programme. Very long tapes tend to have poorer quality reproduction. They are OK for note taking, but not acceptable for broadcast purposes.

You must always announce your intention to use the machine. Recording people without their knowledge is unethical and illegal. Tell your interviewee that you do not have shorthand, and you do not want to get anything he or she says wrong, so this is your method of note-taking. What you tell the subject of your interview is quite true. But using a tape recorder has another major advantage: it frees you to focus tightly on the subject, instead of sticking your head in a spiral-back notebook. Your interviewee should be flattered by your attention and how fascinating you find him or her.

When doing an interview with someone who is famous, never assume that you can remember a lot about them and that you had better not bore them by putting them through their tombstone details yet again. In the first place, what you know about most people you have gleaned from newspapers, and they have been known to get it wrong. Newspaper bloomers are self-perpetuating. Cutting services embalm the error in libraries, and eager journalists approaching the story afresh come upon the relic and introduce it in their own piece. Before long, it attains the status of Holy Writ. It is very simple to ask a celebrity gently about his background details. A formula I have found helpful is, "Look, Mr X, I know all sorts of things about your career, but I want to get this exactly right, so could I pretend I know nothing at all, and start from there?" That way you get around the difficult spot where you really do not know anything about Mr X, but do not want to offend him by saying so.

Having double-checked the current facts/myths about the subject, it is then up to you to ask them something new and different about themselves. The late Richard Burton was once asked to do an interview, and, wearied by the entire thing, said he would only do it if the supplicant journalist won the job by asking him, on the spot, some question he had never been asked before. The journalist spoke.

"Are you good in bed?" she enquired.

Burton—fair play to him—laughed and gave her the interview. She later made a book out of interviews with the famous, all starting from that point.

While on the subject of interviewing, it is worth a small digression to answer the question many newcomers to writing ask, which is: "How to you get someone to agree to be interviewed?"

If the "victim" you fancy as a potential interviewee is ex-directory, you have to use initiative and work hard. If he is a star, appearing in a particular theatre, then the theatre will probably have the name and hotel of his manager, and that's what you should ask for. Somehow "Could you give me the name and phone number of Rod Stewart's manager?" sounds more suave than "Please can I talk to Rod Stewart?" It's also more likely to pay off.

One of the problems about famous people is that they often

don't wish to waste their time on a "maybe." So they ask you what publication you write for. And you say "Well, eh, I hope to place this with eh…" and they say thanks, but no thanks. The way you get around this is by asking some pal on a newspaper (if you haven't got one, get one) if they'd be likely to buy an interview with X if you were lucky enough to get X, and then telling X that the paper is interested.

Whatever way you put it, it tends to be a vicious circle. Paper doesn't want interviewee unless he is well known, interviewee doesn't want to be talked to unless paper guarantees interest, you can't satisfy one without first satisfying the other. As with all vicious circles, the laurels go to the person who can break through dramatically, and for no good reason anybody can spot. I remember on one publication for which I worked, being fascinated when an unknown writer appeared from nowhere with a bundle of tapes under her arm, all of them interviews with major figures in the world of politics. To this day I know not how she got them, but I do know where they got her—up the ladder, fast.

Another freelance friend of mine landed an interview with an international star by thinking laterally. He watched the arrival of the big car to take the star away.

On the side next to the curb were thousands of fans, fighting for the opportunity to get close to the star. In the middle of them was the star, and he was flanked by heavies whose job it was to prevent journalists getting close to him and make sure he got, on his own, into the back seat of the car. What the freelance observed was that there was nobody on the other side of the car. He opened the passenger door on the other side and got in.

"We'll be going in thirty seconds," he told the driver, who shifted into first by reflex. The freelance leaned across the back seat, opened the door on the curbside, called the star by name and indicated it was time to go. The star, who was used to responding to first name inputs from people he did not know, had no problem in using this as a cue to get into the car. The heavies piled in after him and into the following car, and within a minute they were on the open road. At that point, my friend introduced himself and the star was so amused by the effrontery shown that he gave him an interview, there and then, on the back seat of the limousine. Complimented on achieving the impossible, my freelance friend shrugs.

"What's the worst that can happen you if you get pushy?" he asks rhetorically. "You get refused or you get thrown out. So? What have you lost? And, on the other side, there's always the chance you might win."

If you do win an interview, then reward the interviewee with total, fascinated attention, and try not to be predictable in your question areas. The worst insult you can earn is when an interviewee says to you "I'm always being asked that question." The best compliment is when someone stops dead and tells you that not only have they never been asked that question before, but they've never thought about the matter raised. If that happens, shut up and let them do their thinking and talking on the spot.

An interviewee, famous or anonymous, should get the feeling that he has your total, undivided, warm, positive attention. And you should have his attention, too. Find out if you can when he has his next appointment. It can be awkward to be just working up to the key questions when the interviewee looks at his or her watch and decides that he's given you more than enough time.

Being warm and positive does not mean that you cannot ask difficult questions. Read Jessica Mitford's *Confessions of a Muckraker*. She summarises the method whereby the interviewer leads gently into the more challenging questions, and is amusing about how one of her former students caught her by the short and curlies merely through using the technique she had taught him. If you have to ask a difficult question, you do not have to make a major production out of it. Remember, always, that it is the *answer* that is going to appear in your feature. It is the answer that is of prime importance. So if you want to ask a man how he lives with himself after selling his daughter into slavery, there's no point in doing a command performance. Shout and roar at the man and he will walk out.

Ask the same question with wondering gentleness, and you are likely to get a super—and very usable—answer.

I do not believe that there is a question an interviewer cannot ask. In my time, I have had to ask people about their sex lives, their terminal illnesses, their personal failures, their enemies and their tragedies. I have never had someone refuse to answer a question, which is what interviewers are always afraid of. What *has* happened to me, and is much more difficult to cope with than an straightforward refusal, is where an interviewee begins to weep. One woman talked to me about the drug addiction of her teenage son, and, as I probed the problem, tears began to flow. One's instinct is always to pull back. I kept going. So did she. She subsequently wrote to thank me for the feature I had written—and for the fact that I had listened to her and not shut her up.

"Most people are embarrassed," the letter said. "Even doctors just want the facts. They don't want you to cry or tell them how desperate you feel. I know you were asking difficult questions, but I didn't mind that."

Never dress up personal cowardice as sensitivity directed at other people. Many freelances are poor interviewers, because they are too concerned with their own sensitivities and capacity for embarrassment.

"I felt she'd be upset if I asked her questions about that aspect of her story," they'll tell you. "So I just moved on to something else."

Interviewers, even those interviewing for the print media, should be aware of Robin Day's excellent Code for Television Interviewers:

1. The television interviewer must do his duty as a journalist, probing for facts and opinions.

2. He should set his own prejudices aside and put questions which reflect various opinions, disregarding probable accusations of bias.

3. He should not allow himself to be overawed in the

presence of a powerful person.

4. He should not compromise the honesty of the interview by omitting awkward topics or by rigging questions in advance.

5. He should resist any inclination in those employing him to soften or rig an interview so as to secure a "prestige" appearance or to please Authority; if after making the protest the interviewer feels he cannot honestly accept the arrangements, he should withdraw.

6. He should not submit his questions in advance but it is reasonable to state the main areas of questioning. If he submits specific questions beforehand he is powerless to put any supplementary questions which may be vitally needed to clarify or challenge an answer.

7. He should give fair opportunity to answer questions, subject to the time-limits imposed by television.

8. He should never take advantage of his professional experience to trap or embarrass someone unused to television appearances.

9. He should press his questions firmly and persistently, but not tediously, offensively, or merely in order to sound tough.

10. He should remember that a television interviewer is not employed as a debater, prosecutor, inquisitor, psychiatrist or third-degree expert, but as a journalist seeking information on behalf of the viewer.

When you tape-record an interview for print purposes, you should hold it for at least four weeks after the interview appears in the paper. Interviewees have been known to swear blind they never made a particular point, and when that happens the interviewer will be rescued only by the recording. The same applies to notes, including original shorthand notes.

When you have interviewed your subject at length, and have a transcript of what was said, the next task is to make a feature out of it. Later in the book, you will find guidance about how to write a number of features which may incorporate an interview. It is also possible that you may have a market for a simple transcript; some magazines favour the Question and Answer approach to an encounter with a personality. In which case your job is already done, and all that remains is to write a cover letter and put a stamp on the envelope. (And on the SAE).

For the moment, however, let us just look at what I believe is the most interesting possible outcome, in print, of your interview: the personality profile. The constant appeal of, and market for, the personality profile comes about because this is the feature which introduces unknown aspects of a famous person to the reader and which enhances the reader's knowledge of the subject's appearance, history and views.

A good personality profile, inevitably, is based on someone famous. That is a basic pre-requisite. The four essential building blocks of a good personality profile are these:

- Biographical Details

- Quotations

- Descriptions

- Judgement

Biographical Details
Let us define biographical details. They are the details of a human being's life, not the details you put on a tombstone. Chronological dating is boring. It is not what happens to a man, but what he does with what happens to him that is important. It is not the commonality of his experience that is exciting, but the characteristics and the crises which make his experience, his family and his life individual. Whenever you find yourself telling the reader that your subject went to a particular school in 1943 and graduated a few years later, you should stop

yourself. You are concentrating on scaffolding, not on building. The reader wants to know about successes and failures, crises and challenges, triumphs and disasters, learning and losses. You must build all of those in such a way that they become much more impelling than the scaffolding.

Look for inconsistencies. If an interviewee tells you all about 1965, 1966, 1967 and 1979, then in 1968 he was in prison or hospital or somewhere else worth looking at. If you are told that in a particular year he changed career direction, the important thing is not the day, month and year, but the person or people who influenced him to make the shift, the factors that persuaded him, whether they were money, prestige or boredom in the earlier job, and the kind of person he was at the time, physically and mentally.

It is often helpful to elicit the biographical details of an interviewee's life in chronological order, but it does not follow, as day follows night, that you must subsequently frame your profile along the same lines. You may choose to skip great chunks of material that are fascinating to the interviewee, but would spell boredom for the reader, or you may choose to start in the present tense and do frequent flashbacks. The key thing to remember is that your biographical details should illustrate the reasons why the famous personality is the person he or she is today.

Although biographical details should never be allowed to move centre-stage, they must be accurate. Central to such accuracy is advance research (when this is possible—it is not essential) good note-taking and checking of details ("you did say you were up an Alp that Christmas, didn't you?") and faithful delivery of these accuracies into the final feature. Those with access to newspaper files have an advantage in the research before the interview takes place. Most of us have poor memories—ask any group of people to give the full names of all of the first men to set foot on the moon and it's wall-to-wall blank faces. So a look through journalistic files can help to provide reminders. Not that such files should ever be accorded Biblical status. Journalists make mistakes, those mistakes find their way into print and are calcified forever in files to mislead researchers. Never import a fact without checking its status with the interviewee.

Check everything, but do it in a non-theatrical, brisk way. Although I have covered, earlier in this chapter, the essentials of interviewing, it is worth pointing out that many novice freelances waste a lot of creativity on the framing of questions they plan to put to personalities. Impressing the interviewee with the style, depth or insight of a question is not the object of the exercise. The objective is to get together an interesting body of fresh material on the subject, and the questions most effective in achieving that are simple unimpressive—and effective. In any good interview, it is not the question prepared in advance which winkles out the significant answers, but the good supplementary.

If a personality is used to self-presentation, the chances are that a spiel has been developed, which inevitably tends to focus on successes or triumphs. The question, based on good listening, which probes the years not stressed by the subject, is the one which will produce the goods. The follow up question of "Why?" or "Why do you say that?" may push the interviewee beyond an obvious or banal first statement into something more vivid or considered.

Having elicited biographical details, you should try to insert them on the run. Not

>"He took a B.A. degree in Oxford in 1966,"

but

>"An Oxford B.A. launched him into the mid-sixties, with the hope of…"

Finally, be wary of introducing biographical details with repetitive phrases.

Never send a piece to an editor which has three sentences, the first of which begins

>"In 1966, he took a degree in Arts in Oxford,"

is followed, two sentences later by

>"In 1968 came his first opportunity to join,"

and, four sentences thereafter, by

"In 1974 he got his first chance at -"

Quotations

A personality profile without quotations is essentially an essay on the person being profiled. It is a quite legitimate form of journalism, but it puts the personality in a fairly static role which does not allow him or her to speak. A profile must allow the reader to hear the personality speaking. In his own language.

The latter is important. There is a world of difference between a tidied-up paraphrase masquerading as a quotation and the real thing. For example:

A   "I cannot accept the death of my son," she said. "His possessions in my home are a constant reminder."

B   "I'll never accept it," she said. "I'll never accept Jaimie's death, not as long as I live. His books, his briefcase— everything that's still hanging around the house just jolts me every day."

The second is neither grammatical nor elegant. But it was the way the film star talked to my student. A was the way my student had tidied it up—even though she had the tape recording of the star's actual words. Get people the way they really talk. Those who know the subject you have profiled should say to you afterwards:

"I could *hear* him saying that thing about angling. It's exactly the way he talks."

Do not kid yourself that you have a quote when all you have is a snippet. Here is a snippet in ineffectual action.

> She talked haltingly about her son, Jaimie, who died at seventeen in a car accident. She recalls him, she says, daily, when she sees belongings of his "hanging around the house."

A snippet is too short to allow us to hear the real voice of your interviewee, and too imprecise to allow us to differentiate between your interviewee and all others. Give us good big chunks of quotations, and attribute them simply. People usually say things or comment things. They don't rebut or refute or retort or smirk things. When attributing quotations to the speaker of the quotation, the best advice to the writer is arguably the legend you can read on American badges: KEEP IT SIMPLE, STUPID! Or KISS! for short.

Once you have established the voice of your interviewee, and you have also made it clear that nobody else is speaking, then you can insert perhaps the fourth block of quoted material without a separate attribution. Just indent it, as you will indent all quotations, put quotation marks around it, and leave it alone. So, if you were inserting in the fourth or fifth paragraph of your feature about Terry Prone the point I have just articulated, this is the way you might do it:

> If you have established the voice of your interviewee, and you have also made it clear that nobody else is speaking, then you can insert perhaps the fourth block of quoted material without a separate attribution. Just indent it, as you will indent all quotations, put quotation marks around it, and leave it alone.

If you get really good, thought-provoking quotations, you can use one of them as the introduction to the whole feature. If you get a really good summary quotation, you can use it as the last element in the feature.

Descriptions

The profile, when it appears in print, may or may not have a photograph with it. If a photograph appears, it may show the person in stasis, or the picture may be ten years old. Either way, it will not establish the physical impact of the subject in the way good descriptions can. Good descriptions are the opposite of the details frequently broadcast before news bulletins, where the police seek missing people on the basis of details which defy the most imaginative person to visualise a human being. Missing persons may be of stout build, ruddy complexion and be dressed in black jackets with brown shoes, but personalities need to be described in ways which put them in the centre of a brightly lit stage: moving, talking gesturing, reacting.

The existing public perception is the ideal starting point for any feature about a famous personality. The writer can choose to prove the public perception wrong ("You think this guy is a weedy little twerp, and he's really a super intelligent six footer") or to confirm, or, in confirming the perception, provide added facets to it. Describing someone is a skill which is best informed by kindness.

An otherwise excellent feature was wrecked for me by an opening sentence which said:

"Father Joe Bloggs has long brown teeth."

I had known Joe Bloggs for years and he had the longest brown teeth I had ever seen. But as the opening to a feature? Come *on*.

On the other hand, when a writer profiling me described me as Junoesque, everybody got the message that I was very fat. She did a professional job of physical delineation, but she halted one step short of brutality.

Judgement

This is the single most difficult thing to achieve in a feature, but it must be achieved. The reader must, at the end of your profile, make a judgement on the person being profiled. Does the reader like him or dislike him? Find him amusing, interesting, stimulating, pompous, small-minded, witty, self-absorbed or superficial? In the course of interviewing the personality, you must be making judgements yourself, because if you are not, what you are preparing is not a personality profile but a Public Relations Puff Piece; you are taking on board everything the personality wants you to take on board and getting ready to regurgitate it for the public. Your approach must never be one of the PR person dutifully transcribing the statements of the great in an aura of appreciative awe. Your posture may be warmly supportive, but you do not have to switch off your scepticism or your discrimination.

However, having made your own judgements on the person you have interviewed, you must not then lay those judgements on the reader. You must show the reader, not tell them. You are in partnership with the reader, not with the personality, but you must assume, as part of that partnership, a capacity in the reader to draw inferences from the implications you may subtly stitch in to your feature. You must present the reader with the information which led you to develop an impression of the personality.

If, for example, the personality talks a great deal about the importance of family life, and how he values his wife and children and appreciates them as important individuals with their own lives and skills and talents, yet in the course of this he never mentions them by name, you may make the judgement that he is a self-serving poseur and that you are dead sorry for his wife and kids. You should not say that in print, however, because, quite apart from the possibility that he will sue, there is the added fact that you are robbing readers of an important reader's function: making up their own mind.

Finally, a word of warning.

The subject of a personality profile is, generally speaking, the only one who should be centre stage. Unless the writer of the profile is himself or herself so famous that sharing of the spotlight is legitimate, the reader will not want to know about the writer's fears, domestic problems or reactions to what is being said. Bluntly, you are not important enough to be in it. Keep yourself out of it.

The Dos and Don'ts of getting a personality profile right are:

DOS

• *Do* let us hear the personality speaking in his own words.

• *Do* give us a sense of what they look like.

• *Do* give us the material on which we can make a

judgement about them.

- *Do* get the facts right about them.

- *Do* make sure that your readers share your sense of presenting a personality on a brightly lit stage.

DON'TS

- *Don't* record what the personality says and then paraphrase it.

- *Don't* tell us what to think—let us make up our own minds.

- *Don't* do a PR puff piece. Give the personality to us, warts and all.

- *Don't* give us tombstone details. Give us details of progree and setback.

- *Don't* give us old stuff.

Chapter 5

Travel and Columns

> Your Manuscript is both good and original, but the part
> that is good is not original and the part that is original is
> not good.
>
> Samuel Johnson

The features pages of a newspaper are made up of all kinds of
categories of writing, including:

- Funny Material
- Personal Experience Accounts
- Travel
- Columns
- Consumer Education

    Special Expertise.

Can *you* write under any of these headings? If you can, will
you place the pieces?

Let's try to answer those questions by going through the
categories one by one.

Funny Material

Funny material is always in demand and always in short
supply. The first time I came across a feature in a newspaper by

Erma Bombeck, I innocently asked where she lived, assuming that it was around the corner from where I lived, since the feature had been cleverly edited to take out any specifically American references. Told that she was a syndicated writer who appeared in newspapers all over the world, I then wondered aloud how it was her work was so widely purchased. The Features Editor said crisply

> Because syndicated material is cheap. Cheap and arrives on time and is of consistent quality. Every fool in this country can write *one* funny piece. It's producing a funny piece every week that's the real challenge.

Nobody can teach you to write funny material, but you can learn the habit of mind that turns the obvious on its side and examines its kicking legs. You do that by reading the funny writers of today and yesterday. Stephen Leacock. Robert Benchley. Dorothy Parker. (Especially the last, although she did not write features at all. The mistress of the one-liner, she was the woman who commented that if all of her friends were laid end to end, she wouldn't be a bit surprised. Her poems and short stories are odd and sad and funny.) Reading Benchley and Parker underlines a reality worth underlining: writing funny stuff is not easy and is highly competitive. Both were members of the "Algonquin Round Table," a group of wits and writers who met at lunchtime in the Algonquin Hotel in New York to exchange *bon mots*. To survive at the round table, it was not enough to be merely witty. You had to be witty *right now*.

Not all of the funny writers dealt with newspapers. P.G. Woodhouse, dubbed "the English language's performing flea" by Sean O'Casey, had a genius for piling the ordinary on the ordinary and ending up with the outrageous. Ireland's John D. Sheridan had a gentle quirky way of finding fun in events that are common experiences and rarely noticed as funny by the people going through them. John Lennon tinkered with words to make them amusing, and Tom Wolfe, when he writes semi-documentary material like the Electric Kool Acid Test, as opposed to his more recent fiction, is hurtfully funny at the expense of real people. *The Secret Diary of Adrian Mole* is funny enough to have been a success, in translation, with Moscow schoolchildren.

There are as many ways of being funny as there are ways of being serious. There are only two drawbacks. One is that the funny things that happen to you are not necessarily funny in print. We have all had the experience of someone coming to us, bubbling with the humour of an event which has just befallen them. We give them all our attention and they give us all the details, and at the end, we can see why they laughed when it happened to them, but it does not leave us doubled up and helpless.

The other drawback is that what seems very funny to the writer and his/her family may not seem very funny to an editor. But, remember, a rejection slip does not mean that the piece does not work; only that the piece does not work for the editor it was planned for. It may be funny, but may not tickle his individual funny bone. Or it may be similar to something he is already committed to buying from a syndicate, like, for example, Erma Bombeck features. Bombeck churns out columns every week and bestselling collections every year, all based on the premise that self-derogatory examinations of domesticity by a beat-up mother and wife are funny. They can be. They can be. But an awful lot of unsuccessful features get written about how little Johnny stuffed his mother's bra down the toilet or how husband of put-upon wife complained that she didn't iron his shirt properly or how the dog got hold of Mommy's anti-histamine medicine and was sick as a—well, fill in the gaps yourself. These features are unsuccessful for one of several reasons:

- They don't catch people's attention, because they waffle at the beginning instead of getting quickly to the point.
- They lack pace.
- They are self-serving or self-conscious.

- They have too many peripheral details in them.

- They are too like too many other features on the same theme.

- They don't ring true.

- They go on too long.

If you have a talent to amuse, then you will quickly find a market of people willing to be amused, in newspapers, magazines and radio programmes. But remember that most of them would rather have a steady supply of even material than the odd burst of spectacularly funny stuff, and so you need to be constantly on the lookout, not for funny things that happen to you, but for things that happen to you, or that you observe happening to other people, that can be made to be funny. Note-taking is important. Oddities find their way into a note-pad and have a way of breeding there. My mother, a market researcher out one day asking questions about shampoos, encountered a man who said he had never washed his hair in his life, on the basis that furry animals didn't wash their fur, they just allowed nature to clean it by wind and rain and occasional immersion in the sea. My mother wanted to talk cats at this point, but didn't, mainly because she was looking at this man's soft, gently shining hair and wondering if she could believe him. In due course, as it turned out, his claim was corroborated by his wife, who added, for good measure, that he never washed his feet either. He had a theory about that, too.

That incident sat for two years in a notepad before I could figure out a way of crafting a funny feature around it. The same note-pad today reveals all my jottings about my son's comments at various ages. When he was four, he watched the elephant at the zoo for a long time and then observed that the elephant *crept* around. Most people assume, wrongly, that elephants thunder around. They creep. Watch one. Later, he commented on a film star of somewhat less than striking looks that she had "an uneventful" face.

The great thing about kids is that the way they observe things can make those things funny or make a writer look at them in a new way. Also, because they are innocent, they don't charge royalties when parents and friends steal and publish their one-liners.

Whatever about eventful faces, you do not have to have an eventful life in order to write funny material. It can be made of the most ordinary daily happenings. One of the pieces I wrote ten years ago and still see re-printed every now and again was an off-the-top-of-the-head job about dreams. Dreams and nightmares. Everybody has them, every night of the week. Short of material, I wondered if I could be funny about them, in response to a request for a feature from the editor of a religious magazine.

When he had first phoned me I had been more taken aback than excited.

"I couldn't write on religion," I said.

"I don't *want* you to write on religion," he told me. "I'm drowning in stuff on religion. People send it to me by the cartload every week. I run a magazine which is brisk, ecumenical and socially concerned. I go for short features. Less than a thousand words. What do they send me? They send me four thousand word sermons on outdated religious matters, overly pious and written in heavy, purple-passage type prose. That's what they send me."

"I see your problem," I said, trying to de-fuse his suddenly growing rage.

"No, you don't see my problem," he retorted. "Because it's a religious publication, they also don't send SAEs, because they think I won't be mean enough not to send them back. But I am."

"You am what?"

"Mean enough. I never send them back. And I'm beginning not to answer phone calls either. They ring me up and argue with me when I don't use their stuff, do you know that? They lecture me."

An important consideration, that. When you have submitted

a piece (WITH SAE) to an editor, after enough time has elapsed for you to be sure that it has actually arrived on his or her desk, you lift the phone and ask about it. Just checking, you say lightly, that you did get a piece from me about the mating habits of rhinos. Oh, you did? Oh, excellent. Anything I can add? Any information you might want? Do you think it will meet your current needs?

If you have sent a piece which has a limited shelf-life, then you have an even better excuse for ringing. Hi, Mr. Features Editor, I sent you a piece on making your own chocolate Easter eggs, and I'm just checking that you got it, to make sure you have a chance to assess it while it could still be useful to you... In making these phone calls, you must be positive, up-beat and setting out to solve the editor's problems, never your own. To that end, you should have in your hand a list of alternative features, so that if the editor says "Nah, this doesn't suit us at all, I wouldn't be seen dead using it," your response is not a silently slashed wrist or a wild torrent of abuse, but a calm "Oh, well, could I just run another idea past you, because I think it just might be of interest. You know there's a growing trend for..." The same thing applies if the editor likes your piece. Be ready to build on that foundation. Oh, shucks, you're going to print my thing about guard dogs? Thank you. Marvellous news. D'you know what I was thinking might be a worthwhile follow up...? Barracking or reproaching an editor because your piece is being rejected is the one sure way to guarantee the rejection of further pieces and a constant unwillingness on the part of the editor to come to the telephone to discuss anything with you.

If you think you can be funny, the most likely markets are in the evening papers and in magazines. Morning and Sunday newspapers tend to confine their comedy to brand-name staff funnymen and women.

Personal Experience Features

- You are on a plane when the pilot cannot get the wheels down and makes an emergency landing with all passengers physically and mentally braced for disaster.

- You develop an unusual or life-threatening illness.

- You are mugged in mid-day in a crowded street.
  You fail an exam.

- You have a fight in a shop about shoddy goods they refuse to take back.

- You are unemployed and constantly humiliated by the lack of response to letters of job application and by the experience of job interviews.

If anything like this happens to you or to your friends or family, you have the making of a personal experience feature. What is important is not the event as it happened to you, but the writing of the event so that it is interesting to other people and moves them. The kind of response you are looking for is where people say to you afterwards "I knew exactly what you were talking about," even if they have not had the particular experience about which you wrote.

When writing personal experience pieces, there are a number of pitfalls to be avoided. One is seeking for generality. You are worried that because the experience you write about happened to your child, and she is a middle class city kid of twelve years of age, therefore parents of country working class kids who are younger will not identify with the story as told.

So you fudge the details a bit. The kid is of specifically urban indeterminate age. You water down the quotes a bit so that particularly city slang is not used. You take out details about cars and telephones for fear of offending people who do not have one or the other. What you end up with is pale mealy characterless porridge with which *nobody* identifies.

The rule is that the more specific, the more individual, the more singular, the more demonstrably unique a story is, the more people extrapolate from that story to a wider, general picture, and the more they apply the lessons of that story to their own lives. I read Steinbeck's *Of Mice and Men* when I was about ten years of age. I knew nothing about mental handicap. I knew nothing of hobos. I knew nothing of America's Deep South. I had never seen a gun. I am not sure I had ever even encountered a real live mouse. Yet the story broke my heart and showed me ways of seeing things I had never known before—because it was so very singular. Steinbeck knew that everybody can relate to a real live individual, but nobody can relate to a generality.

Which is not to say that one's individual prejudices, preferences and idiosyncrasies have to be dragged into a personal experience feature.

On the contrary. The most deadly introductory phrase (apart from the eternally untruthful "to make a long story short") is "I am the kind of person who…" It invariably introduces a trait generally shared but not worth boasting about, and presents it as if it was unique and, *ipso facto,* extraordinarily significant. If a jumbo jet accidentally landed on your roof, we really do not feel a compelling need to know that you are the sort of person who irons her tea towels, or that you have a habit of saving teabags to put on your hydrangeas. The only excuse for the presence, in your feature, of such detail, is if you happen to be in mid-tea towel or mid-teabag when the airliner strikes.

Remember the rule of "Show, not Tell." Personal experience features are often about highly emotional subjects, and set out to involve the reader's feelings. That is not done by telling the reader in great detail how you felt at every stage of the incident. Where possible, show the event and let your feelings be deduced and shared by the reader. As happens in a feature sent to me when I edited a woman's magazine. The feature was about a premature baby and his weeks in an incubator before being released to his family. Having built up a picture of the tiny big-skulled baby behind the plastic, surrounded by pulsating machinery and connected to different coloured tubes, the writer, who was the child's mother, tells the story of receiving a phone call from the hospital saying that on her next visit, she would be able to take her preemie home.

I put down the phone. Colette, my four year old, pranced

92

beside me.

> "Was it the hospital?"

I nodded.

> "Is our baby coming home?"

I nodded.

> "Are you glad?"

There was a silence.

> "Are you glad, Mammy? Are you glad?"

I looked at my hands to see if they shook. They were   still.

> "Of course I'm glad," I said, beginning to believe it.

Without telling us about every emotion she is feeling, the writer has let us know that she is fearful and unsure about the prospect of coping with the delicacy of the baby, and yet determined to manage the challenge. When you write personal experience features, you must be wary about of telling the story faithfully, the way it was, as opposed to telling it so that it grabs and holds attention. Let us say, for example, that you are writing about a serious family illness. It actually started, and you can remember this in great detail, with your partner feeling a bit off. Not major league sickness. Just a bit off. That was eighteen months ago. Two months after that, he began to feel a bit tired. As time went on...

Forget it. Long before we find out what ails him, we will have lost interest in him.

If, on the other hand, you start at the crunch point, you have some chance of hanging on to your reading audience:

> They told him on a Tuesday it was cancer. That   Tuesday made sense of the previous eighteen months, and cast doubts on the coming eighteen months...

Never assume, when writing any kind of feature for a newspaper or magazine, that you have introductory time at the beginning. People read first paragraphs not as introductions, but as *qualifiers*. It is the first paragraph that decides them to keep reading or suggests to them that they should skip this and move on to the one beside it. So if your story is about falling down the stairs and breaking both your legs, do not give us all the tedium about the alarm clock going off, about you getting up, cleaning your teeth, making the bed, and heading across the landing, unless you have a way of telling these everyday hum-ho matters which makes them riveting. Remember that party bore, the man who tells you he has something fascinating to tell you, and then tells you he must first just put it in context. Ten minutes later he is still laying down foundations and you are planning, Mafia-fashion, to incorporate him in those foundations.

If you are the person the incident happened to, be fastidious in the way you portray yourself. Don't get in the way of your own story. If you tell it well enough, readers will almost feel it happened to them. They will not feel that if you ladle on irrelevant personal details. Be honest, too. Never portray yourself as having only the acceptable emotions, or behaving impeccably. In a crisis, most of us say things we should not say, think things we should not think—and those are what should appear in the feature, not a sanitised, cosmeticised self-serving edited version.

The incident itself does not have to be tragic or rare. A minor car accident, the death of a pet, the hurt of peer pressure or bullying are all common happenings, but one person's lively pointed anecdote can make any one of them stand out. In short, you do not have to live an exceptional life in order to have great material for personal experience stories. Checking back through the sales of this kind of story made by trainees on Basics of Journalism Courses I ran, I find themes covered include:

- Weight loss of 40 pounds. Why the writer was overweight in the first place, how people treated her when she was obese, what was the catalyst provoking the decision to diet, the trauma of deprivation, the diet and the end result.

- Becoming a runner. How one middle aged man took to the road, became addicted to "runner's high" and worked up to a marathon.

- Getting a hearing aid. How the writer's family eventually told him that his deafness was more of a problem to them than to him. The examinations, technology and costs involved in selecting the right hearing aid. The difference it made to his life.

- A bee sting that nearly killed. The writer's sister was stung in the throat by a bee and almost died in the following hour, because of a major, fairly rare allergic response. Medical lessons emerging from this incident also featured.

- How I learned to listen. Starting from a doctor's instructions which, not fully heard, were not obeyed, the writer produced a revealing piece about his own lack of listening skills and the exercises he had developed to force him to pay attention to others.

- Late starting. The writer decided, in her forties, to learn how to play the piano. Her feature examined the difficulties and joys, the comparisons with children doing the same exams, the failures of starting late.

- Buying a lemon. This feature told the story of a car which, from the moment of purchase, gave trouble. It was funny, informative about consumer rights, and named names of garages and manufacturers.

- Building a swimming pool. The writer and his wife decided to make a swimming pool from scratch. Neither of them had even built a pond before. The saga ran to three instalments of 1,200 words and was worth every syllable. At the end of it, you knew how to build your own swimming pool and you also knew that you would be out of your mind to try.

- A scar from childhood. This quite short piece dealt with the trauma of incest. Presented to a newspaper under a pseudonym, it was published by that paper with an introductory paragraph explaining that this *was* a false name and why the paper was taking the step of using it.

- Not loving the baby was also published under a pseudonym, because the experience had already caused the writer such difficulty. It was a simple feature which suggested that instant bonding between mother and newborn is not an unfailing rule, and when it does not happen, the pain and sense of inadequacy this causes the mother is massive.

- Becoming literate. The writer of this piece had come to my course having first spent two years learning to read and write. He was forty-two, and could make you laugh and at the same time touch your heart with anecdotes about how clever the illiterate become at concealing their inability to read.

What all of the features had in common was an absence of spleen-venting. When someone writes a feature with a view to taking revenge on people who have wronged them, the end result is usually unreadable. You must stand back from the hurts of your own life if you want to make them mean anything to other people. Some people can have a ghastly experience and immediately stand back from it, writing without involving their own innards messily in the process. Other writers need to make a note of their intention to write about a particular stinker and then postpone putting words on paper until the volcanic rage associated with the stinker has died away.

Marketing your personal-experience story depends on the experience and what market it is likely to fit into. Some newspapers like features about human trauma. So if you have survived major injuries in a car accident, they would like to know about it. Some newspapers like features which throw a human interest slant on a social trend. So if you can deliver a feature on how it feels like to be unemployed, and how you fill the task-less day, they are likely to be intrigued. Some magazines are ever-open maws for stories about family illness and childhood trauma.

Before you submit your self-revealing feature, do a bit of scenario planning. Assuming that the publication buys the feature and wants it run under your name and with your picture, will you be willing to have this happen? You may suddenly have second thoughts in the privacy department, as you realise that your gory personal details or the gorier personal details of your wife/child/best friend are going to be spattered all over the daily paper.

At that stage, you may undergo an attack of the anonymities, wanting the feature attributed to "Our Special Correspondent," and illustrated with a silhouette drawing of an unidentifiable but bravely tragic something or other. At this point, the newspaper to which you sent your piece is liable to get cross (because you have not planned your submission professionally) and is also liable to lose interest, because an anonymously-told tale never has the same appeal to a daily publication as one that has a by-line of a real live human being.

Long before you submit a feature, work out the impact it will have on your own life and the lives of those around you. Other people can be extraordinarily sensitive about having their lives publicly paraded, even if it is in a way which does not seem to you, the writer, to be particularly defamatory. The worst cropper I came over a friend's privacy was when four of us spent a night playing some board game. Not Monopoly, but something along the same lines. It was a new game, designed to provoke role-playing among the participants. The four of us role-played our way into the small hours with a mixture of aggression and comedy which, told the following day in a brief feature, captivated my editor and the readers of the evening paper for which I was then writing. I did not use surnames in the feature, just first names. The other couple involved in the game felt that I had taken what was essentially a private sharing of fun and sold it for public consumption. They did not speak to me for several years. It taught me a lesson. Do not make assumptions about other people's willingness to be incorporated in your personal experience material, no matter how light or inoffensive that material may be. On the other hand, you should not write the feature (or any other fact-based prose) with one eye on the other people who may have been present when it actually happened. If they are too easily identifiable, and you know that they would not want the story told where they can be identified, think about selling it overseas.

Although the writer has been described, accurately, as "someone who is always selling somebody down the river," if you have a story to tell which is too painfully personal to people who are too close to you, you may have to write it and keep it. Never postpone putting the words on paper, but use your discretion about putting the resultant prose in the mail. Pat Conroy, best-selling author of *The Water is Wide* and *The Great Santini,* says that he could not publish *The Prince of Tides* until after his mother was dead, because enough of the novel was based on his own family experience to have caused her enormous problems if it was published while she was still alive.

One final thought. Be wary of libel. Just because you remember something bad that somebody did does not mean that you can incorporate this happily into something that will see the light of day in print. The *Writers' and Artists' Yearbook* gives you the basics about avoiding libel. Read it before someone takes you to the legal cleaners.

Travel Writing

The last of the turkey is scarcely consumed when the first of the travel brochures begin to fall in the letter box, suggesting that this year, holidays should be spent in Inner Turkey or Outer Mongolia, unspoiled Connemara or wonderfully spoiled Manhattan. The magazines and newspapers, particularly the Sunday newspapers and their associated magazines and colour supplements, develop a parallel hunger for good travel features.

But what defines a "good travel feature"?

It helps if it is about a place that is not already over-exposed.

If the only place you have travelled to is Torremolinos, then your chances of publishing a travel feature are small, unless you have the capacity to make readers see that resort as they have never seen it before, either because you have happened upon some local oddity (tangerines crossed with bananas to produce a completely new fruit, pottery made from crumbled seashells or slave labour imported from some other country during the high season) or because your style is magical.

Whenever you travel, take a camera with you and learn to take good quality pictures, both black and white and slides (print film is not so good for reproduction by newspapers or magazines). Make notes. Deciding that something is beautiful and memorable is a mistake. You will remember it too vaguely, unless you have access to notes that will recall the texture of what you saw or experienced.

Reading travel features and books about travel is arguably the best training to enhance your competence in an over-supplied market. Journalists love to be appointed travel correspondent of their newspaper, because it means free trips to exotic places. People who never write about anything else want to write about travel. Many publications (although not all of them) see the text in the travel pages as no more than the peg on which is hung a great deal of lucrative advertising. You have to be very, very good to establish a reputation as a travel writer and find a continuing market for your wares—but it is worth the extra effort it takes to be very, very good.

That extra effort means:

- **Avoidance of travel-writer's cliches**
  If you don't know what these are, you don't know where to start. Find them and learn to avoid them.

- **Honesty**
  If you get a free trip, say so. It gives the reader the knowledge by which to judge what you say about the location.

- **Do the sums**
  Find out what everything, whether it is a glass of Coke or a leather handbag, costs in the resort. Do not stop there. Make the effort and translate the foreign currency into the currency of your own country, so that people understand,

before they get there, what the expenditure on predictable items is likely to be.

- **Do not show off**
  Most people are nervous about travelling. Do not make them feel small by implying that you knew from birth what to tip a Venetian gondolier. Enable your readers to feel at home in the resort about which you are writing when they eventually go there.

- **Be topical**
  If an international incident has just happened in the place you are writing about, mention it if you are writing for a newspaper, but not (because of the longer lead time) if you are writing for a magazine.

Writing A Column

When you go to the supermarket, you know the whereabouts of the things are that you particularly like. If you are into canned asparagus tips, you could find your way blindfold to the shelves where they lurk.

If your preference is for sugar-free cereal, you can get to it without thinking twice. If you have a passion for a particular brand of instant coffee, you will not only locate the shelf, but the position on the shelf where that brand is always to be found. The supermarket tends to keep brand-name goods in the same position, to reinforce the feeling of comfort among regular customers.

It is the same story when it comes to newspaper columnists. They are always in the same position in the paper, and always in the same position in the reader's mind. The reader will turn to a columnist to be pleased—or, equally important, to be irritated. Columnists contribute an identity to a publication. The longer they have been with the publication, and the better they are at their job, the less willing the newspaper is to see them go. If a Tom Wolfe, a Jimmy Breslin or a Russell Baker leaves one newspaper and joins another, it says something about the publication they have left and something about the one they have joined, although it has never been proven that readers in substantive numbers follow a migratory columnist.

The good side of being a columnist is fame. Maybe limited fame, but fame all the same. Fame when they put your picture at the top of the column with your name underneath it, when people summon you to parties and receptions, and when you are invited on radio and TV programmes as a tame pundit.

The bad side is filling perhaps a thousand words every single week. It sounds easy when you set off, but it is not easy to maintain, especially when, as happens with many columnists, you are required to file your copy a day in advance of the rest of the paper, and can therefore be pre-empted by events. Another factor which complicates the life of a columnist is a roving brief. Theoretically, this is a major boon.

"Hey, you mean I can write about ANYTHING?" new columnists shrill.

The problem is that the wide open blank spaces can, in time, give a columnist a distinct case of writer's agoraphobia. In addition, all of the by-lined journalists in every other area of the paper have touches of territorial imperative, and get edgy— sometimes vocally edgy—when a columnist impinges on subjects they consider to be their personal property. The columnist mentions a television programme recently seen; the TV critic gets wrought up. The columnist does a column on a political figure; the political editor gets shirty and claims that he was just about to do a profile on that precise person. The columnist goes on a thousand word excursion into the bad value of a recent purchase and the editor of consumer matters sends a stiff memo.

You pays your money and you takes your choice as a columnist. You can base your writing on the passing parade or you can base it on material on which you have particular expertise. The latter approach is sometimes used as a device to get around NUJ rules. (See Chapter 12).

Where the NUJ refuses membership to someone, there is a loophole which allows that someone to write about their particular area of expertise. You might be a doctor who still practises, and so the NUJ will not allow you to double-job and will not grant you membership of the union.

On the other hand, they may concede that you can be allowed to write as long as what you write about is related to medicine. Medicine and healthcare can be stretched to cover an awful lot of subjects, and so it may be worth an editor's while to go along with this restriction. Other columnists, who do not need to use this device to cope with NUJ requirements, base their material on special expertise, such as, for example, as knowledge of information technology. Increasingly, newspapers require columns from people who can write about standards and proprietaries, interactive systems and computer viruses, and someone who can produce the goods with a reasonable degree of literacy and wit can mark out a good niche as a high tech columnist. Other "data-driven" columns include gardening, bridge, fashion and gossip.

There is a fine line to be negotiated, in writing a column, between having a strong ego and being grossly egocentric. Readers will only take so much parading of personal opinions, expressed as personal opinions.

If you think you can negotiate that fine line, and if you believe you have what it takes to be a good columnist, give yourself a couple of tests. For starters, write a list of what your first 12 columns would be about, and ask somebody if they would be interested in reading those topics. Then, on several different mornings, pick up your newspaper, read it and write a column reacting to an event covered in it—against a pre-set deadline. Examine your conscience about your hunger for personal publicity. Are you happy to have your face smiling out above everything you write, so that your spouse becomes an adjunct and your kids are got at in school?

Once you have moved the obstacles out of your way, put together a couple of demonstration columns and a letter indicating where this column might fit in the editor's existing pattern, and try to meet the editor to explain precisely how what you have to offer would meet his/her requirements.

Consumer Education

Readers do something else as well as read. They buy. They buy food. Drink. Wallpaper. Medicines. Beds. Calculators. Education. Entertainment. Travel. Each one of these purchases calls for information and decision-making. Mass media provide much of the information on which consumer decisions are based. So you would like to be the freelance writer who writes the consumer features? Then you must first assess yourself realistically to see that you have the right natural inclinations.

Good consumer writers are:

- Methodical in their research and note-collation.

- Punctilious in their attention to detail.

- Sceptical (not cynical) about information provided by PR departments. They double-check.

- Low on ego; the product and the logical analysis of cost and benefit are much more important than the writer's identity. You want photographs, by-lines and permission to sound off, go for a columnist's job, not a consumer correspondent's.

The best consumer writer I know produces questions like scattershot in response to every task. One feature she was called upon to write was about fountain-pen devices for delivering insulin to the bloodstream of diabetics. Before she talked to the manufacturers or to the leading expert on diabetes, she had a list of questions:

When were these pens developed?
What advantage have they over injections?
What disavantages?
Do they only suit particular kinds of diabetes?
Do they only suit particular personalities?
Do they only suit particular ages?
What are their dangers?
What is diabetes?

How do you get it?
Can you prevent it?
How does it affect general health/life expectancy?
How does it affect lifestyle?
Is it hereditary?
Is it your own fault?
What's the history of the disease?
When was insulin discovered/invented?
How is it made?
What does this pen cost and how does that compare with injections?
Can you get it anywhere in the world?

Out of that list of questions came a feature which took this shape:

Paragraph 1
Description of man taking fountain pen out of breast pocket in a restaurant and, unnoticed by lunch companions, sticking its point in his thigh, through fabric of trousers. Mystery solved; this was no fountain pen. This was the latest in diabetic technology.

Paragraphs 2 & 3
Diabetes the disease. A hundred years ago, you died of it slowly. Development of insulin. Two types of diabetes. Seriousness of the disease, complications.

Paragraphs 4 & 5
The pen. How it works and what it costs. How it is used best by highly motivated adults and why this is so. Ease of use—but marginal difference in management of illness. Comparisons on a number of points with injection model of therapy.

Paragraph 6
Summary; it may not be for everyone, but it's a high-tech breakthrough. If you are a diabetic, talk to your GP or specialist about whether it would be helpful in your particular case.

Before she submitted this feature to her regular customer, a daily newspaper, the writer rang up each of the sources and read aloud to them the quotations she was attributing to them, and her interpretation of the data they had given her. She says

> When I'm writing a personality profile, I don't read them anything in advance of publication. My first responsibility is to my editor and to the readers. I cannot allow an interviewee to tell me he'd prefer if I didn't portray him this way or that way. On the other hand, when we're dealing in facts, it is essential that I bullet-proof my story at every point.

Some major overseas publications have a complete staff of checkers who isolate the facts in every story submitted and double-check them. This, curiously, does not make life any easier for a really responsible journalist, because knowing that your work is to be checked by somebody else tends to make you more, rather than less, careful. You do not want to be caught out by a checker in some preventable blooper.

Nor is this specialist-checker system proof against failure. On at least two occasions in the past five years, it has been found wanting. One occasion was when a writer based in Spain wrote a marvellous location piece about Vietnam after the war, which was commissioned by an American publication and duly printed by that publication. The writer based in Spain had, sadly, not left Spain in order to write his location piece, which was cobbled together from other people's writings and his own recollections of a decade before, using creativity, rubber bands and spit. The other public failure was when a young woman won a national award for a story written about the tragedy of child drug-addiction, centering on the personality of a pre-teen whose life was examined in much evocative detail. Because sources were confidential, this one got past the checkers and it was only later that the entire story was revealed as fiction masquerading as fact.

Consumer journalism never permits of a short cut, as I was told, again and again, when I shared a job with a formidable consumer researcher. The job was a radio review of supermarket prices, and was done in tandem because the radio programme concerned had massive listenership and the supermarket item was, accordingly, potent to the point of having major commercial influence. On one occasion, we peeled the green skin from potatoes which should not have been dressed thus in the first place, weighed the end result, compared the relative amounts shaved off different brands and did an item about the health implications of green-skinned spuds. Twenty minutes after the programme carrying the item went off the air, we had a phone call from a tearful supplier who had just lost a contract worth a fortune on foot of our report.

My fellow researcher on that job was like the characters in the old spy movies who never took the first taxi that offered, on the basis that it was likely to be filled with murderous assassins or counterspies. She would never take the first bit of information that offered. When items on the shelves failed to carry price labels, she would wander off, can in hand, and accost a passing staff member.

"How much?" she would query, waving it.

"Fifty seven pence," the staffer would reply, and I would be ready, pen in hand, to write the number down. My companion, however, would be wandering off in a quite different direction, to accost an assistant manager and ask him the same question. She frequently got a radically different answer, which both invalidated the first as a usable fact and also gave us a little extra slant for our story. Similarly, when we would be pricing baked beans, she would take the price of the can in front, then burrow away to the back and then go off to one side. Only when she had three identical brand cans of baked beans weighing in at the same weight and priced the same, did she allow us to write down that price as a fact fit for public consumption. That double-checking was tedious. It was also what kept us out of court when people got litigious. And people get litigious on consumer reports more often than they get the common cold.

There are, however, some areas of consumer reporting where opinion is at least as important as fact, and that is reportage on the experience of eating out. You can do this anonymously, so that the table in the restaurant is never booked in your name and no *maitre d'* ever knows you by sight. Or you can be high profile and visibly terrifying. What you cannot be is ignorant or tolerant. One of the best known international food commentators holds that if you do not know the principles and practice of the major world cuisines, then, as a food journalist, you have the unjustified dogmatism of the person who says they don't know much about painting, but by God, they know what they like. Tolerance is another major disqualifier. Some of the best cookery writers hold pens dipped to elbow level in vitriol.

There are, of course, many other feature areas in newspapers and magazines for which you may have a particular aptitude.

Horoscopes are a permanent feature of many magazines, and (this is a secret, don't tell anybody) are often hacked together, not by an occult "expert" but by whoever on the magazine staff or among its freelance contributors wants to do it. It is an easy number, although it rarely pays well.

Advice, on the face of it, looks easy to deliver. That was certainly the view of the writer I picked as Agony Aunt on a teenager's magazine. Except that after six months, she needed her own agony aunt, because the material coming to her was so monumentally depressing, because topics she felt should be raised, because of their educational value to young adults, never seemed to surface, and because I had indicated to her that I wanted lightness of touch to distinguish this feature, and coping with unwed motherhood, youthful drug addiction, incest, poverty, pornography and exploitation tended to add a touch of lead to her mental state and writing style. Agony Aunts, increasingly, are people who have training in counselling and who see themselves as public information and health education resources, as opposed to majoring on entertainment along the lines established in Britain by Marjorie Proops and in the US by twins Abigail Von Buren ("Dear Abby") and Ann Landers.

Knitting is like a good river. It goes on forever. So many publications have a slot for a knitting column, which is often provided to them free of charge by knitting pattern publishers. This suggests that if you design knitwear and would like to peddle patterns, you might be better off doing it directly to the yarn suppliers. A word of warning, though. Knitting may not seen of world-shattering importance to you, but if a magazine runs a knitting pattern and accidentally leaves out one line of the pattern, there is an avalanche of enraged mail and cries for compensation. Before a magazine will consider you as a supplier of knitting patterns, it will need to be assured that each of your patterns will work out precisely as they should, and that you have double-checked each stitch.

Cooking is a difficult area to get into. Everybody thinks they can cook. Everybody and her husband think they can write about cooking. Once a cookery writer achieves a position with a newspaper or magazine, they tend to stay there forever and to live to a great age. Patience, persistence and some unique advantage are required if you are to sell yourself into this area. (I have wanted all my life to write about cooking, and nobody has ever let me.) If you get an opening, cherish it, and by that I mean that you should take the care over your recipes that they deserve. No recipe should ever be recommended in print which has not been tested three separate times. A hint worth passing on is that one cookery writer develops a recipe, then hands it to her daughter-in-law on paper, and her daughter-in-law tries out the instructions. The collaboration serves the purpose a control-group serves in medical testing; if the daughter-in-law produces a different end result, then it's back to the chopping board. Ditto if she cannot follow the instructions -

many cookery writers use words like "braise" and "infuse" without ever giving a thought to the moron like me who assume that "braise" is a misprint for "bruise" and, in misplaced obedience, knock hell out of a dead chicken as a first step to a cordon bleu dish.

Flower arranging, Bridge, home decoration, car maintenance, etc. It is quite possible that there is a hidden need for a regular feature on a subject not covered up to now. Do a summary of the kind of feature you would like to do, indicating length, frequency and style, and incorporate that summary in a proposal to an identified editor, stitching in the incredible benefits to his publication of having such a feature. Give him reason to believe that you can deliver a series, as opposed to an initial flurry, and, if you can find an example of where this kind of feature has been used by overseas publications, give him an example of how it has worked elsewhere.

When planning to assault the world of newspaper features pages and of magazines, you should be aware that there are some major differences between them. Magazines appear less frequently and have a longer lead time than do newspapers. They also take longer to pay, and vary greatly in size of payment. Some pay tiny amounts. Some pay heartwarming chunks of cheque. Some pay a little to some people and a lot to others they know and appreciate. In the beginning of a career in writing, it is often fun just to have something of yours in print, whatever the payment, or even if the publication pays nothing at all. Later on, being paid a decent rate for the job is important and "negotiable" can be a hurdle to be surmounted. The determining factor should be your own valuation of your time and your computation of how long the job takes. One writer I know has costed her day at £100. If the job takes half a day, she charges £50. If it takes two full days, she charges £200. That would be pretty hefty by freelance standards, but the writer concerned is good, and knows it. She gets less of the small-time work, and more of the interesting stuff. Whenever work is thin, she will run up a feature under another name, submit it from a different address, and take a smaller fee in order to keep herself going.

That sort of situation is enviable. Editors will often get away or try to get away with paying the lowest possible fee for work. The exceptions are made in the cases of reliable professional writers who know their own value.

The National Union of Journalists (see Chapter 12) has branches catering for freelances, and those branches regularly bring out guides indicating the agreed minima to be paid to writers for features of a specified length and type.

A major problem for impecunious writers is how to find out if a magazine used the material sent to them. There is no simple answer to this difficulty. Some magazines are slow responders. They hang on to articles forever, and, as a result, are the bane of every writer's life, because you don't know whether your piece has been used, and they are just not paying you, or if it has fallen down the back of the editor's desk.

This is a situation which improves a little as you go on, partly because it is less of a gamble as you get wise to the ways of particular editors, and partly because some magazines, if you become a semi-frequent contributor to them, will be sent to you as complimentaries, so you will be able to follow your progress or lack of it, for free.

In the absence of a free copy or of a payment from a particular magazine, there are two avenues open to you. Check by telephone that they have got the piece, and leave it for a while. Just how long "a while" is varies. For newspapers, the general rule is that if they haven't used it within a month, it's unlikely that they will use it. For magazines, that nail biting interval is longer by a fortnight or more.

While you are waiting, you can take the other avenue, which is to become a browser cum buyer in some leisurely but comprehensive magazine shop, where they do not employ women in nylon coats to walk up and down behind people too poor to buy the publications, saying loudly "No reading the magazines, please." The occasional small purchase will keep one of these shops happy, and you can check on all the magazines to which you have sent material. If you notice that your piece has been printed, and that an unreasonable length of time has intervened between printing and payday, send a civil note, giving details of the date of publications and your own whereabouts, and request payment.

Feature writing is fun and keeps a lot of wolves from a great many doors. To make a success of it, watch the dos and don'ts:

DOS

- *Do* appreciate the different between funny and facetious. Comedy is saleable, smartass is less so.

- *Do* keep the features coming. The more frequently your material arrives on an editor's desk, the more likely he is to think of you when he wants a regular column supplied.

- *Do* follow up features submitted with a civil phone call.

- *Do* see your life—and the lives of those around you—as source material.

- *Do* remember that ideas are everywhere.

DON'TS

- *Don't* invade other people, exposing their privacies in a way they could not have expected. If someone is not in the public eye, they may tell you things as a friend they would not like to see attributed to them in a newspaper. Find out what their feeling is first, before you submit a piece based on their experience.

- *Don't* rely on your memory when you have an idea. Write it down. Don't lose the bit of paper.

- *Don't* use features for revenge.

- *Don't* be exploited. Value your time and have respect for your writing skill. Don't, once you know your business, work for someone who pays you little or nothing.

- *Don't* feel you have to establish the same relationship with all editors. Some editors are warm, supportive, civilised people. Some are red in tooth and claw. When you meet one of the latter, don't take it personally.

Chapter 6

Writing Books

A person who publishes a book appears wilfully in public with his pants down.

Edna St Vincent Millay

The lure of the greasepaint and the smell of the crowds have nothing on the hypnotic attraction of writing books. Creative writing courses over the years have always come electrically alive when the possibility is raised of getting something between hard (or soft) covers. The questions come pouring out:

- Where do you start, if you want to write a novel?

- I've often read bestsellers and thought "I could do just as well as that."

- Can you make a living at it?

- Is it all right to fictionalise your own life story?

- Do you need to get an agent first?

You start writing a novel when two things come together: your idea of what a novel should be, and your sense that you can produce that. If you believe that a novel should be a coruscating construct of language and glancing images, then you cannot start writing that kind of novel until you have the skills to deliver both. Each of us has our own definition. One worth listening to, if only to react against, is that of the late John

Gardner, a critic, poet and novelist who, before he died in the early eighties had specialised in the teaching of creative writing. His detailed account of the creative process, entitled *On Becoming a Novelist,* looks at the proposition thus:

> Normal people, people who haven't been misled by a faulty college education, do not read novels for words alone. They open a novel with the expectation of finding a story, hopefully with interesting characters in it, possibly an interesting landscape here and there, and, with any luck at all, an idea or two—with real luck a large and interesting cargo of ideas.
>
> Though there are exceptions, as a rule the good novelist does not worry primarily about linguistic brilliance—at least not brilliance of the showy, immediately obvious kind—but instead worries about telling his story in a moving way, making the reader laugh or cry or endure suspense, whatever it is that this particular story, told at its best, will incline the reader to do.
>
> We read five words on the first page of a really good novel and we begin to forget that we are reading printed words on a page; we begin to see images—a dog hunting through garbage cans, a plane circling above Alaskan mountains, an old lady furtively licking her napkin at a party. We slip into a dream, forgetting the room we're sitting in, forgetting it's lunchtime or time to go to work. We recreate, with minor and for the most part unimportant changes, the vivid and continuous dream the writer worked out in his mind (revising and revising until he got it right) and captured in language so that other human beings, whenever they feel like it, may open his book and dream that dream again...

A wide-ranging definition like that would have terrified me into impotence before I wrote my first short novel. By way of counterpoint, let me tell you what happened.

A television producer had his attention drawn to a script of mine by an altruistic mutual contact. He liked it and rang me up. I was to write him a television play immediately. I did as told. The producer accepted the play, but, being rigorous and combative by nature, challenged every line of it to achieve motivation for various actor's moves and plot developments. After one of what I had grown to think of as his interrogation sessions, I muttered aloud that I should write a bloody novel to show him what was going on in the characters' minds when they took particular courses of action. Having muttered it aloud, it made sense, and I wrote the novel.

Internal changes within the TV studio then resulted in my play not being produced. They paid me and shelved it and several other plays. So I sent the novel which came about as an explanation of the motives of my *dramatis personae* to a publisher and nine months later had a slender hardback in my hand.

There is no magic starting point for a novel. Or for a best seller. Barbara Taylor Bradford, who has had a string of international bestsellers, says that she has no idea, when she sits down at her typewriter, if the book is going to sell in millions or if it is going to fail to sell a copy.

> All I have is a story to tell about a number of characters who are very real people to me. I knew I wanted to be a novelist when I was a child in Yorkshire. I had no brothers or sisters so I invented playmates and told them stories.

Taylor Bradford says that you start a novel by starting a novel. You simply sit down and start writing. And you don't expect it to be easy.

> Writing novels is the hardest work I've ever done. The salt mines, really. I sit long hours at my desk, starting out at six in the morning and finishing around six or seven in the evening. And I do this six and a half days a week, till my neck and shoulders seize up. I make tremendous social and personal sacrifices for my writing, but after all, I chose to be a novelist. Nobody held a gun to my head.

Evan Hunter, the man who writes "serious" novels under his own name and police procedurals, including the 87th Precinct series, under the name Ed Mc Bain, was once a literary agent, and he takes a numerate, rather than a literate, stance on how you get started:

> First of all, determine how long the book will be. The average mystery novel runs about 200 pages in manuscript, but a straight novel can be something as slim as *Love Story* or as thick as *Gone with the Wind*. You are the only person who can figure how many pages you will need to tell this story. Take out your calculator. Are you writing a 300 page novel? OK. How many chapters will you need? The length of each chapter will be determined by how much you have to *say* in that chapter. if you're depicting the Battle of Waterloo, it might be a trifle difficult to compress it into ten pages. If you're writing about a man putting out the garbage, you probably have only a scene and you'll need additional scenes to make a full chapter.

So, whatever approach you adopt, you get started, and you write a novel. The next question is, can you sell it? Novels get written because novelists cannot not write them. They get published by an unpredictable combination of luck and judgement and they get read because of marketing, placement on the shelves, personal impulse and the direction of the wind on a given day.

Based on all of these unpredictables, it is not surprising that in most English-speaking countries, a mere handful of writers make their living solely through the production of novels. These are the cream of those whose novels are accepted by publishers; lower down are the vast bulk of the would-be novelists whose manuscripts come back each time, more tired and more dog-eared. Yet one of the most doggedly held ambitions among writers is to produce and sell The Novel. There are many writers around who make tidy little sums regularly by contributing non-fiction to magazines, newspapers or radio programmes, who regard all of this writing as marking time until they get to write their novel or put together their volume of short stories. If you ask them about money, they will tell you that perhaps when their book is published it will make a packet and they can retire.

The reality is that first of all, your novel may not be published, in which case you will have wasted something like 70,000 words worth of energy, since, whatever satisfaction the thing gave you to write, the real satisfaction is in seeing it printed. The *first* real satisfaction. The more important satisfaction is the lurching surge of pleasure you get when you see a perfect stranger reading your book on a bus or a train or on a park bench. There is a secret ecstasy attached to being an unidentified witness at other people's enjoyment of your work.

If your novel does make it on to a publisher's list, then it will be fighting for shelf space and for the attention of readers with so many others that it will be lucky if its sales are in the hundreds. The average Irish novel by a first time writer hardly ever becomes a bestseller in hardback. The return from those sales is not going to put anyone on easy street. If, therefore, what you have to say does not have to take the shape of a novel, if it can be broken down into dozens of small magazine pieces, then, from a purely financial point of view, you would be better off channelling your creative energies in that direction.

There are, nevertheless, numbers of writers who would be much happier to be poor but have a book with their own name on the spine of it in their bookshelves, than be rich and have a folder of magazine cuttings. There is a mystique about books which almost every other form of publication lacks. In addition, there are writers whose work will not readily take any form other than the novel.

Publishers, on the other hand, tend to be less interested in novels than in other forms of writing with surer returns. Producing a hardback (or indeed a paperback) novel is vastly expensive. Here is where the larger British and American publishers have an advantage over smaller publishers; they have a much bigger market.

To produce one novel may be enormously expensive, but to produce thousands of millions is proportionately more economic, and to sell in those numbers makes the operation less of a hopeful leap in the literary dark.

On this side of the Atlantic, many publishers are not madly

eager to see novels submitted, but loth to turn them away. All work submitted speculatively is carefully read and, if good enough, considered for publication. Just remember that you have competition and lots of it. One large general publishing house, which does not bring out very much fiction, finds an average of twenty unsolicited novels on its doorstep every year. Of those twenty, on average one is considered worth taking a gamble on *in the entire year*. That's a strike rate of .01%.

In America, the situation is very different. Talking to the Senior Editor in one of the larger publishing houses there, I found that the direct submission of manuscripts is actively discouraged.

"A manuscript which was sent in the mail would never get to my desk," she told me. "The boys in the mail room would turn it over, see if there was a return address on it, and send it off on the next mail."

"Without even opening it?"

"Right. Why would they open it?"

"To read it?"

"Oh, no. If your manuscript does not reach us through a recognised agent, we would not read one word of it."

"Why not?"

She gave a life-is-too-short shrug.

"Not enough time. I don't have enough time to read the books sent to me by agents I personally know, so how could I read speculative submissions? None of us can, and it's corporate policy to send them right back. They should check, anyway, before they waste their dollars on mailing it."

I have always yearned to have a literary agent, because, like many writers, I have a great relationship with inanimate objects like pens, paper and word processors. It's only people give me problems. I want an interesting job not meeting people. For that reason, I would love to put words on paper, shove the result in an envelope addressed to a literary agent, and have that agent doing the market research and the hard-sell. The key factor which today has prevented me seeking an agent in a more active way is a realisation that few agents actually sell manuscripts.

Most of them maximise what can be earned by a sale which would probably have happened without their intervention. Richard Curtis, who has been a top literary agent in New York for over twenty years, makes the modest claim that having an agent tips the odds in the author's favour:

> The chances of culling a saleable manuscript out of the piles of material submitted each week by non professional authors are much better for an agent than they are for a publisher. The reasons that an author may write a perfectly publishable book but then submit it to a perfectly unsuitable publisher. If you turn out a nifty formula western and send it to Knoff, Harper & Row, Crown Scribers and Altereum, for instance, it is most likely it will never see the light of day. But if you submit it to an agent, the agent will say 'Of course it's wrong for them; they sell and publish that stuff. But it might be right for Doubleday or Ace or Dell or Barton, publishers that love western lines!' The agent, in short has many more options with a given manuscript than a publisher does. But *you* have a problem, and it's a fundamental one. You need an agent, but an agent may not need you. Despite a stark surge in the last decade in the number of literary agents entering the field, few are so hungry for business that they take on new clients indiscriminately. First of all, because they have been (unofficially, but effectively) vested by publishers with the responsibility for separating literary gold from dross, their reputation would quickly be ruined if they took on everything that comes their way. And, second, they don't have time to read everything that comes their way, at least not without a staff of readers.

However, if an agent takes you on board and likes a submitted manuscript he will take it to the publishers who deal in that type of book, putting personal credibility and belief in your book on the line. This counts for something with a publisher. In addition, agents negotiate for their clients when it comes to fees for serialisations and spin-offs.

No reputable agent will charge a fee for reading a manuscript or trying to market it, and you would be well-advised to ask for it back from those who do. The percentage of your royalties that goes to the agent is regarded by many writers as a worthwhile investment. One novelist, however, told me that after four years of being represented by an agent, he had abandoned the whole thing and begun to represent himself, and was much happier with the results.

If you want to find an agent, then the *Writers' and Artists' Yearbook* will provide you with an up-to-date list with names, addresses and areas of special interest. If you write to the Society of Authors' Representatives at P.O. Box 650, Old Chelsea Station, New York, NY10113, enclosing a stamped self-addressed envelope, they will send you a list of reputable agents in the United States. Make sure the stamp on your SAE is American and of sufficient value if you are writing from the other side of the Atlantic.

Whether you try to sell your book at home or abroad there are a few points which are worth consideration. One is that certain types of books have been written too often. Christopher Derrick, a publisher's reader whose *Reader's Report on the Writing of Novels* (Gollancz, 1969) should be on the shelf of every aspiring novelist, has a long list of novels that are cliches and turn publisher's readers off at source.

Fifth on that list is what he calls the Painfully Irish Novel, and he sums up its elements thus—

> Glory and heartbreak of wild uproarious youth in Dublin, with students and poets and poverty and fine whirling talk and Guinness and the Gardai and people being sick at parties, and mad-eyed mistresses and dotty peers, and great crumbling Georgian mansions where pigs loiter in the drawing-rooms and everybody hallooing off into the night in some overloaded rackety old car, while the inescapable Church hovers over all.

Enough said.

Another kind of book which looks to the writer like a cast-iron bestseller, and which frequently does not sell, is the book written to a popular formula. If this year's bestseller is a book of riotous reminiscences by an observant nursery school teacher, then you can bet your last ha'penny that hundreds of people are going to sit right down and write their funny memories of the classroom.

The problem here is that the gap which elapses between the conception of the original idea, and the publishing of the clone, or follow-up book, is usually too great. If book A appears now, it is unlikely that book B can be brought out in less than fourteen or fifteen months, and by that time the vogue for that particular kind of writing may have died. If a week is a long time in politics, fourteen months is a very long time in publishing. There are other difficulties too—you may think the formula is dead simple, but the original writer may be better at it than you are. A great many people can point gleefully to the paper-thin quality of Harold Robbin's plotting and conception, but he has sold millions of books and his imitators do not.

Whatever the theme of your novel, it is by the actual writing it will be judged to be publishable or worthy of rejection. Anyone who does any reading of fiction knows that there is no single style which, once a publisher's reader has taken a glance at it, will signal publish me to him or her like the bottle which invited Alice to drink it. Quiet reflective novels get published. Rowdy extrovert novels do, too.

The novels which quite decidedly signal "don't publish me" to a reader seem to be those written either by someone with no talent, or someone with no ability to stand back from the work and assess it honestly. The first problem is insoluble, the second can be dealt with by effort and professionalism. Sadly, many novice writers retreat into defensiveness at the first suggestion that their work requires trimming, re-writing or a radical re-think.

"But that's the way it *was*," they insist, revealing their "novel" to be all-too thinly disguised autobiography. The ability to read what one has written, acknowledge that in real life it may certainly have happened, but that in a novel it does not work, is worth cultivating. A good publisher's editor will certainly push the writer through this process. Many writers cannot handle it.

The classic pattern is that the book is accepted, subject to some re-writing, the writer is in the seventh, eighth or ninth heaven and all's well with the world. Along comes the editor. This chapter should come out. That phrase recurs and should be lost. Over here is a non-sequiter. Could we have much more development of this character, who is two-dimensional? This incident is too like what happened in last year's best-selling police procedural—could it be re-written, please? Suddenly, the world doesn't look so rosy, and war breaks out between writer and editor. It may well have been this process that was in Peter De Vries mind when he said:

"I love being a writer. What I can't stand is the paperwork…"

Whether a novelist likes it or not, most novels are extensively re-worked between the time of submission to a publisher and appearance on the book-shelves. If the writer is lucky, the editor turns out to be a wise supportive sensitive person like Max Perkins, the man who nursed along Hemingway, Fitzgerald and several others.

Any potential conflict with an editor can be mitigated in advance if, prior to submitting the book, you first re-read it as critically as you can, watching for and excising any kind of self-indulgence; phrases there for no good purpose other than that they sounded pretty as you wrote them down; characters irrelevant to the thrust of the work. Watch also for facetiousness, and for anything which is contrivedly funny or sad. Read the manuscript as if you were someone else, and assess how the tone of the writer strikes you. Are you being talked down to? Or bossed? Or wooed too obviously.

"One could write twenty books on the dire examples of doomed manuscripts," one publisher told me. "But quite a proportion of them would be OK if the novelist concentrated a little less on being A Writer and more on reading his own stuff with a critical eye."

If you are a writer nobody has ever heard of, then sending a couple of sample chapters to a publisher or agent and providing an outline of the plot is unlikely to result in a sale. They will want to suck it and see a lot more than two chapters will allow them. So first novels tend to get written in their entirety before they are submitted.

You have a manuscript. You will find details in the next chapter on how to turn it into a manuscript an editor or agent will read, delivered in such a way as to ensure it gets to him. Right now, however, let us look at the other kinds of writing which can end up in books.

Short Stories

Short stories give rise to much misunderstanding.

- Some people believe that short stories are a training ground for writing novels. You play around in the short length for a while, and then you go for the big stuff.

- Some people, reading deceptively simple short stories, assume that the genre is easy.

- Some people, having placed a few short stories with magazines, expect it will be easy to have them published in collection form.

Misunderstandings, all of them. The training ground notion is fostered by the experience of some writers, like James Plunkett, who produce, early in their writing career, a book or books of short stories, and later on write a sizeable novel. In Plunkett's case, the novel was the best-selling *Strumpet City*. However, the fact is that the short story, like the sprint, is an entity on its own.

Some short story writers would be betraying their skills and instinct if they were even to think about a novel. Some novelists only broke through to hearing their real "voice" when they abandoned short stories.

As for the publication of a collection of your short stories, don't hold your breath. The market for short stories is constantly under siege, and publishers maintain that very few collections of short stories sell.

"Increasingly, we are seeing writers as *properties*," one publisher told me. "Almost like brand names. If you have a writer who has had a couple of bestselling novels, then you can bring out a collection of their short stories, pushing their name very ostentatiously on the cover, so that what you are selling is 'another from this writer' rather than short stories *per se*. But a collection of short stories by a newcomer can't be positioned like that."

Having short stories collected into a volume is even more difficult to achieve than having them published as individual entities.

Non-fiction books

In many ways, it is easier to have a non-fiction book published than to have creative work brought out. There is an avid market, for example, for text books. If you are a teacher in a specialist area with an ability to communicate the facts about that speciality to young people, you might find that your knowledge could be translated into a book and make you a profit. Most educational publishers are constantly seeking new writers competent to deal with various disciplines.

Many publishers are also seeking writers who can put together factual books about topical subjects, whether they be environmental issues or personal development matters. The key thing is to make an approach to them first to test out their level of interest.

Never, ever write a non-fiction book first and then seek a market for it. The procedure is to work out initially precisely what kind of book you want to write, in what area. Then prepare an outline of what could be covered between the first and last pages, and then submit that outline to a publisher, together with a specimen chapter. Always enclose a big stamped, self-addressed envelope for the return of your proposal if it is considered unsuitable.

Ghosting

To be a ghost-writer, a few years ago, had literary status

equivalent to the social status of the flasher. The image has improved, however, to such an extent that in the US nowadays, ghosting is seen as a major special skill and ghost-writers who help figures like Lee Iacocca to best-seller positions are highly valued and extremely well paid. In Britain and Ireland, the ghost-writer is rather less valued, and publishers tend to prefer to keep the ghost's name off the book, in the belief that it will sell better if it looks like the undoctored outpourings of the famous man or woman.

Ghosting requires self-effacing fascination with others, curiosity and courage. The courage is necessary because when you are ghosting, you have to get the person around whom the book is to be built to be *honest,* and that quality is something of which many political, industrial and showbiz figures have very little experience. Pushing the person to honesty may not be the only problem, however. Anybody who has read Bob Geldof's *Is That It*? knows that Geldof has no problems being honest. He had problems, however, with the ghost writer appointed by his publishers, and eventually wrote the bulk of the material unaided.

Ghosts get their jobs by being known to a particular publisher. Publishers seek professional hacks to do ghosting, rather than inspired amateurs. There is much solid research to be done, much transcribing of interviews, much wading through damn cement on the way to a shiny event, much pushing and persuading to be done so that the person with whom you are working comes across as a real man or woman, despite the fact that most of them just want to appear likeable, witty, successful, good-looking, hard-working saints whose distinguishing figure is their overwhelming modesty.

Collaboration

Putting two writers together no doubt once struck somebody as a way of achieving double the value in half the time. It is never quite as simple as that.

Collaboration is an interesting but not simple challenge. There have been some fairly half-baked attempts, like the volume which still sells, and which incorporates work by eight or nine famous detective story writers. Each picks up the story from where the previous writer left off, and moves it along. The whole thing has curiosity value and very little else.

Collaboration is usually between two writers, and is arguably most successful on non-fiction books, where research is shared then each writes particular sections and they mate them subsequently, or else one does the main body of the writing and the other kicks it into stylistic shape. Writing relationships can be very difficult or very easy. One of the most celebrated and commercially successful relationships of this kind broke up a few years ago with considerable bad feeling on both sides.

On the other hand, some partnerships go on for decades. The two men who, jointly, amounted to the detective story writer Ellery Queen not only produced novels and short stories, but edited collections of other people's short stories and created a publication—*The Ellery Queen Mystery Magazine,* which continued after the death of one of them.

Two of today's most successful collaborators in the detective story and anthology area are Marcia Muller and Bill Pronzini, who describe collaboration as "a unique opportunity for two writers to create something better than either could have accomplished alone."

Children's books
Children's publishing is a difficult area. To be attractive, a child's book usually requires very expensive colour presentation. The younger the reader, the greater the requirement for photographs or illustrations in full colour to help the text along. This kind of book is expensive to produce, and can bomb. Books aimed at those in the immediately pre-teen years are easier to produce because at that stage it can be assumed that the young reader does not need illustrations quite so much.

Those who accept the occasional children's book say that the main fault in manuscripts submitted for this area is that "They're written from a adult standpoint, often by people who don't have a great deal of contact with kids. They're not written the way kids think." If you tell your kids stories and if you have a reputation among friends and relatives for doing it well, write them down now. Postponing it until the kids are grown up mean that ideas and language which were charmingly appropriate will have become just a touch outdated. Where you have a friend who does super illustrations, it may be worth your while to get together with her and produce a sample chapter which would give a publisher or a literary agent the "feel" of the finished publication.

Some dos and don'ts related to breaking into the book market:

DON'TS

- *Don't* plan on making a living from your novel.

- *Don't* set out to write a bestseller

- *Don't* do a name-changed version of your own life story.

- *Don't* seek an agent before you put words on paper.

- *Don't* assume, if your novel is accepted, that it will be published unchanged.

DOS

- *Do* write the novel. Sample chapters are unlikely to sell your book if you are an unknown.

- *Do* stay with the writing with which you are most comfortable. If you're a short story writer, you are not necessarily going to "graduate" to being a novelist.

- *Do* think about smaller publishers.

- *Do* consider non-fiction ideas and submit proposals to publishers.

- *Do* consider collaboration.

Chapter 7

Publishers and Authors

I never lecture, not because I am shy or a bad speaker, but simply because I detest the sort of people who go to lectures and don't want to meet them.

H.L. Mencken

- How do I know what publisher to send my book to?

- How many people at a publisher's actually read a novel?

- If you present a manuscript in the wrong format, will they reject it?

- Surely doing up a manuscript in a perfect format is very costly?

- How important are authors in the promotion of their own books?

Selecting a publisher is a delicate operation. You pick one and you send it to that publisher. You do not send it to several at the one time. Publishers, at least on this side of the Atlantic, hate being put in an auction-type situation. The historic exception to this rule was set some years ago in New York by Letty Cottin Pogrebin, a friend of Gloria Steinem, who set up, with much public brouhaha, an inter-publishing house competition for one of Steinem's titles. This upped the price and upped the value to the purchasing publisher, because of the publicity which accrued.

One of the ways to find out which publisher should be your first port of call is to seek the catalogues of a number of them, on the basis that if you know what a publisher has brought out up to now, you know what kind of books he favours. Most publishers, plied with stamped addressed envelopes, will send their catalogues on request or they can be obtained from a friendly bookseller. From a selection of these, it is possible to pick the firm whose list seems most in keeping with your own work or ideas.

If you are submitting a non-fiction work, your covering letter should indicate how your work differs from books on the same subject.

The publisher's reader is the first person to get a look at it. If that reader says anything remotely hopeful, it then goes to another, and if he/she says anything warm, it becomes a topic for serious consideration. The publisher's reader, therefore, is a man or woman you should keep in mind when preparing your text.

Who are they, first of all? They are not the hostile critics many writers envisage, sitting in the back rooms of publishing houses with hobnailed boots on, the better to stamp on hopeful (or hopeless) manuscripts. Some of them are academics, some writers, some are just people interested in reading who have become loosely attached to a publisher over a period of time. In many ways, theirs is a thankless task. They earn little—it can range between £15 and £75 a book. They have to read a fair amount of drivel. They have then to write a report, usually about a thousand words long. They have the responsibility of saying, if necessary, "this person who has laid time, energy, and probably heart and soul on these pages cannot write, and I suggest you do not publish the book." Few of them enjoy doing that, even though their identities are hidden from the rejected writers. Their identities are also hidden from successful writers; assuming that their verdict is positive, that the book is accepted, and eventually becomes a hit, it is unlikely in the extreme that the publisher's reader will see his name go in front of the public as the man who spotted the hit-maker.

What is important to remember is that publisher's readers are not in the business of being clever about your book. They are not literary critics, who earn their bread by being interesting, entertaining or scathing about whatever is written. The publisher's reader is expected to read the book with an open mind, and then make his report.

If you do not want to alienate him immediately, the manuscript must be presented properly. Very few are. Many publisher's readers spend their lives ploughing through ill-types or even handwritten verbiage on tissue paper. Because no reader wants to be the guy who missed on Mr Tolstoy's first novel, they read even the worst. But they do not have to *like* it.

Witness publisher's reader Christopher Derrick—

> Remember that your name and address will be typed on your title page, and will thus become known to the publisher's reader. Be warned. If your novel is single spaced and typed invisibly and cloggily right up to the edges of your uncomfortably large and ridiculously thin paper, I shall still give it the report it deserves on strictly literary grounds. But I shall also come around to your house one evening and beat you silly with a great thick cudgel.

To preventing that reaction, select the paper carefully. Never be mean about it. For the final, "fair" copy, buy normal (A4) typing paper, and thinner paper for copies. It is expensive but worth it. Send a publisher the top copy and another copy and always, but always, keep a copy yourself. Buy a decent typewriter ribbon and keep the keys of the machine unclogged with a toothbrush or a ball of Blu-Tack, if it is a traditional typewriter. If it is a daisywheel or a golfball, even better. A laser printer is beyond the means of most of us writers, but a pal who will print out the text on one of these de luxe printers is worth her weight in gold. Dot matrix is simply not acceptable. Many American publishers now state unequivocally that they will not read manuscripts submitted on this format. I believe they are slightly behind the times. What matters is the number of dots in your dot matrix. The number adding up to what's technically described as "near letter quality" mean that the type they produce is considerably more readable than that coming from many conventional portable typewriters. However the ultimately unacceptable manuscript in my personal opinion, is one printed dot matrix-fashion losing perhaps 7 dots to take up each letter on that nasty slimy thermal paper.

"Most annoying in my view," says an editor who reads manuscripts every day, "is the manuscript covered in blobs of Tipp-Ex, scribbled-over bits and badly aligned words, lines and letters. Continuous computer-feed paper with perforated edges is horrid, too."

Allow good margins—an inch and a half on either side at least. Gaps also at the top and bottom of the page, please. If you cannot guess where the page ends once it is in the machine, and you don't have one of those snazzy typewriters which tells you when the page is nearly finished, then use the old typist's trick of putting a tiny pencil cross two inches from the bottom of the paper. As soon as you see it, finish your line and stop typing. You can rub the marks out later. Always double space, including footnotes and quoted matter. Never switch to a different size of page halfway through, or to a different typewriter.

Try to ensure that every page of text has roughly the same number of words. This makes estimating overall length much easier for the production department. Many publishers have guides, ranging from duplicated single sheets to attractive little pamphlets, on style, including problems like single versus double quotation marks, spelling, punctuation. These will be sent if you sent an SAE (Gill & MacMillan, for example, produce a 28-page booklet, which, if read and adhered to, would ease the life of both writers and publisher's readers.) The essential thing is to pick a particular style and stick with it.

Number your pages consecutively in the upper right hand corner, and do not start off numbering afresh for each chapter. If you have made an addition between page ten and page eleven, what you do is this. Pick another full sized page (not a little one, because it will inevitably get lost) type the addition, and number the fresh page with both a number and a letter, so that it is number 10A. Conversely, if you have to take out a sheet, page nine (assuming page ten is getting the chop) should be amended to read 9/10.

Publishers differ on the question of clipping pages. Some prefer to see manuscripts arriving in small neat boxes, like the box the typing paper came in originally, without any stapling or clipping. Others would prefer to see them clipped in some kind of way which would make the script easy to read. This does not mean any of the following—

- A folder with one of those hooped metal slips which leaps into place, dislocating the reader's fingers.

- A heavy office folder which operates in one of two ways; open, whereupon all the leaves cascade to the floor, or closed so rigidly that the leaves will only half-turn leaving great lumps of unreadable material under the catch.

- Bootlace ties or brass tacks with mermaid tails pushed through holes in the pages. They tear the clothes and temper of the reader and the pages they are supposed to control.

- Any folder or device usually made to store things in, rather than read things from.

Box your manuscript or staple small batches of it together, but always number it and present it as neatly as you can. This applies in triplicate if you are sending off a manuscript which has been rejected by one publisher already. The Bronte sisters rather endearingly took the package of their returned manuscripts and re-addressed them without ever changing the outer paper, so that the wrapping was a testament to the number of publishers who had already rejected it. It is unwise to rub the publisher's nose in the twin facts that you first of all sent your manuscript to someone else in preference to him, and secondly that someone else turned it down. Change the wrapper, and if the front and back pages have become a little dog-eared, take them out and re-type them.

Each chapter in your book should have a new leaf, and copy to be printed in italics should be underlined. Lower-case words will be printed in capitals if underlined three times, and in small caps if underlined twice. Bold type should be indicated by a wavy line underneath the word or phrase.

When you put your manuscript together, you need a title page first of all. This should have the full title of the book, and your name or pseudonym. There should also be a list of the author's previous books, if any, a dedication (if any), a list of contents, list of illustrations if there are pictures, introduction and acknowledgements. After the text go things like bibliographies, appendices and footnotes.

So there you have your book, collated, presented nicely, packaged tightly, the right postage stamps on it and a copy kept. You entrust it to the post office and wait for a response. They may not be quick readers, you figure, so you'll give them ten days. The difficulty with that is that if you have sent it to a large publisher, they may, as a matter of course, send it to a reader and expect a response, at the earliest, in eight weeks, so that the earliest you, in turn, might hear anything would be about three to four months after you sent the manuscript. If, on the other hand, you send your work to a small publisher, they may take even longer. There is nothing you can do to speed this up. Check to ascertain that it has arrived, move on and write your next book and productively bide your soul in patience.

The even longer gap between acceptance and publication seems inordinate long to writers. It varies, of course. A small publisher, intent on getting out a single title to meet a particular deadline, may have a book out six months after the acceptance letter is sent. A year or longer is average. Why the big gap?

The manuscript has, first of all, to be read and usually returned to the writer with comments and suggested changes. Discussing and implementing those changes take time. The text is then read by the copy editor who may have additional queries on style or fact to put to the author. Depending on the book, it may be necessary to have a technical expert or a legal person to read it at this stage.

After this, the manuscript is read and worked on by the designer/artist. Later both text and layout go to the printers for estimates. This is where the necessity for copies comes in. If you have three copies of a book you can keep one, the printers can have one, and the publishers can retain one, so that editing and estimating can go on simultaneously.

When the estimate is accepted, the book is fitted into the printer's schedule and also into the publisher's publishing schedule. If the latter is top heavy for the season, your book may be held over. If several books, budgeted for, have not materialised, it may well be rushed out.

At an early stage, the promotion/sales departments of the publishing house like to have proofs and jackets (book covers) so that they can alert booksellers and relevant magazines and periodicals. They are likely to show you the jacket design, but not to give you power of veto on it. So even international bestseller Germaine Greer found that one of her books, launched in the mid-eighties, went on the bookshelves in a jacket she truly hated and which she felt, contradicted the thrust of the book. You tell your publisher you hate the cover and you will be patted on the head and told that designers know best. You take a draft cover, show it to people, get unfavourable responses from those people and quote same to your publisher, you have some chance of being listened to.

Once you have sent off the final fair copy of your work, you are left to sweat it out with very little to remind you that you are a budding Author, except a contract. This contract will probably be in unreadable legalese, and so long and apparently convoluted that you will be tempted to sling it in a filing cabinet and forget about it. This is a bad idea. Before you sign either of the two copies (one for you to hold, the other for the publisher's file) have it looked over, either by a literary agent, or by a lawyer.

Apart from clearing the contract with legal people, it's a good idea, if you know any author, to check with him/her if there is anything in particular you should be wary about. It's very easy, for example, to check on the bookshelves which writers have been published by X publisher before, and to check with them if they found any aspect of X's contract particularly exacting.

Generally speaking, a publisher should offer you a royalty of at least 10 per cent of the selling price of a hardback book. 7 per cent should usually be the smallest proportion of the selling price of a paperback offered. This royalty is unlikely to be bigger unless you are an established writer commanding a good market. If it seems a small proportion, remember that 30-40% of the retail price goes to the bookseller, 20-30% to the printer and binder, and 10-20% on sales and distribution, including advertising costs. The publisher supports editors, accountants, artists and books that do not sell as well as he hopes they will. In addition, he sends free copies out for review. So 10 per cent is not bad, and if you are offered less, it is worth considering the possibility that perhaps the publisher is investing his money in your product, at what may turn out to be considerable risk.

However, do not let your gratitude blind you to what rights you are signing away. Publishers' agreements for books which could, conceivably, be filmed, serialised, published in paperback, translated, broadcast or televised should contain provision for all such "subsidiary rights." Many authors like to retain such rights themselves, but publishers often want an interest in them, since they may be their only hope of profit in return for the risk of publication. They should offer at least sixty percent of revenue from such rights to the author as a general rule, unless their contribution to the book counts for more.

A clause governing reversion of rights is also important. This means an agreement that gives rights back to the author if the publisher lets the book go out of print for longer than a specified time.

Remember that the law assumes that the copyright in anything you have written is yours, and that you assign only certain defined rights to publish in particular forms, particular parts of the world and within particular periods. An agreement that assigns the whole copyright in return for a lump sum or an ill-defined royalty is against your interests.

All of this applies to smaller pieces of work. There is no harm, for instance in acknowledging a payment for a short story with the remark that it is in respect of "first serial rights." Indeed, if you do not do this, you could be giving some little magazine an income for life from Hollywood or some other buyer, or unnecessarily forfeiting a further potential fee.

In pursuing this, be business-like but not neurotic. Editors quickly tire of poets who, on acceptance of their eight-line lyric, insist on an agreement specifying that they hold on to Japanese rights. Books publishers on the other hand, should not be cross if you insist on defining your rights and if they do, you can bet they had their greedy eye on some subsidiary right.

Having got all of the legalities right, having agreed to the blurb, provided biographical details and had your picture taken, the next step is Publication Day. Tarantara, or words to that effect. Publication day can be a big razzamatazz day or one you spend quietly in your study thinking lonely deep thoughts, depending on the marketing approach of your publisher. Some publishers like to launch a list, rather than a book. They have a press conference-type event twice a year at which they announce the titles and authors they will be bringing out in the coming months, and it is all very formal and informative. Some publishers, on the other hand, like to have a reception or a party to launch a particular book. They like to invite a tame celebrity to make a speech, and to have the place infested with friendly journalists and hyper-active press cameramen. They like to have their authors signing books in bookshops and being scintillating on radio and television shows.

It is tempting to believe that you should always be published by the second kind of publisher, but this is not the case. Books are arguably the oddest commodity that can be made available for public purchase. Some books that are never publicised achieve a cult readership and eventually a mass readership purely on word of mouth, whereas others that hit the headlines on a foamy upsurge of hype never sell at all.

The classic example of the latter happened in America in 1988, when the autobiographical outpourings of a household name TV star named Vanna White were published. Vanna White is quiz-show glamour. Her publishers availed of every publicity opportunity. She did everything any human being could do in the way of promotion. The book bombed. Three months after publication, newspapers were carrying stories about the publishers having to pulp perhaps 70,000 copies of it.

Hype is not infallible. However, if you can help your book along by nudging it into the public's awareness, this is worth doing. Appearing on radio and television is one way of doing this.

Let's assume that your publisher has set up an interview on a TV chat show for you. With luck, you will have an opportunity to talk with the interviewer before the interview actually goes out, and be told roughly what areas the interview will range over. You will not be told the questions the interviewer proposes to ask, firstly because it is not the "done" thing, and secondly because an interviewer does not know all of the questions in advance—many will emerge as supplementaries to the main line of thought.

Similarly, on many radio programmes, the interviewee will be led into the studio under cover of a disc, and there may be thirty seconds in which to give the interviewer the name and *raison de parler* of the interviewee.

Studios are unnerving, television studios more so than radio studios. The setting, which, viewed on your own television set, seems to have the solidity of Everest, is in fact a feather-light confection of painted aeroboard. Disembodied voices speak throatily out of nowhere, and nobody but the unfortunate novice pays them the slightest attention. Cameras loom up with silent menace, thick pneumatic flexes trailing in their wake, and snaking around the floor in great whorls which seem endowed with a certain horrific life. The lights are scaldingly hot. Everybody seems to be busy, and nobody thinks you are of the least importance, except perhaps the floor manager who, listening to his walkie-talkie unit, will suddenly say loudly and apparently to nobody in particular, "Mr Smith looks a bit washy, doesn't he, Ann?" Ann ignores him, or maybe is one of the throaty voices in his earphones (which they call "cans" just to confuse you). You try to look less washy, and the floor manager suddenly announces that there is less than a minute to go, signature tunes well up, strange signals are exchanged, your heart lodges snugly behind your uvula and stops. The floor manager then suddenly flings an arm at the presenter as if he wanted to shoot him, and the presenter, catching the paramilitary spirit of the occasion, machine-guns you with some opening question.

If you have gone into the studio coasting on the comfortable assumption that "they'll ask me the right questions," it is at this point that you come unstuck. The interviewer may never have read your book, or may have decided that what's interesting about you is not your book, but your previous job as gold-fish breeder. If you wait for the right questions, they will not come, and the interviewer will quickly develop a dislike for you because you are making with the monosyllables instead of sparkling and being expansive.

Before you go on any television studio, decide what you want to say. Not what you want to talk about—that's too vague and general. You might decide that the four most interesting things are:

- Your decision to write a novel after years of non-fiction. Terror. Problems.

- Your choice of a controversial subject about which to write the novel, and the research you had to do to get it factually accurate.

- The story of the light plane landing accidentally on your roof in the middle of chapter 3.

- The film that's being made of your book, and why you don't think Robert Redford is good-looking enough for the part he has agreed to play in it.

Talk out those points to yourself a number of times, and then, when you go into the studio, listen to the questions that you are asked, answer them, and try to get to the little bits of added value that you feel you can offer. Remember, too, that radio/TV time is deceptive. You will be convinced that the interview ended after three minutes when in fact it went on for six. So get to what you want to say quickly, vividly and memorably. Never sit there looking at the compere and expecting him to *make* you interesting. That is a task you must undertake for yourself.

If you are being interviewed several times on TV and radio programmes that have overlapping audiences, please go to the trouble of developing different anecdotes and points for each of them. Nothing is more infuriating to a listener than to hear you on three different programmes saying the same thing. This does a disservice to your book and will not help its sales. Personal publicity requires commitment and hard work.

It is also (like signing books in a public place) extremely invasive, and some writers will not have anything to do with it. Philip Roth assessed the positives and negatives thus:

> On the pendulum of self-exposure that oscillates between aggressively exhibitionistic Mailerism and sequestered Salingerism, I'd say that I occupy a midway position, trying in the public arena to resist gratuitous prying or preening without making too holy a fetish of secrecy and seclusion...

Even if you turn out to be a star of stage, screen and radio, and, in the process, push your book onto the bestseller lists, how soon you can expect to see money coming in is another variable. One school of thought holds that you should stick out for the maximum possible advance. This is a sum paid before publication to writers. It is, in fact, a slice of potential royalties, and it is given in advance on the basis that a book, once accepted by a publisher requires extra work and that this work needs to be subsidised. The drawback (aside from the possibility that a small publisher may, quite simply, not be able to offer it) is that later on your royalties are correspondingly smaller. How often royalties are paid depends on the administrative system of the publisher. Some pay half-yearly, some only at the end of their financial year.

One way of taking your mind off money worries at this stage is to get on with another book. It is also a way of enhancing your reputation with your publisher, who probably has an option on your next work as part of the contract with you.

"When you accept the first book from someone, it's generally because you believe they show talent," one publisher told me. "If you find, after you've accepted it, that they're already at work on their second book, that shows professionalism. You know then that you've got yourself a real writer."

The dos and don'ts of book presentation and self-presentation are essentially these:

DON'TS

- *Don't* use dot matrix printing for your manuscript—unless the end result is near letter quality.

- *Don't* use thermal paper.

- *Don't* use single spacing or narrow margins.

- *Don'* t do media promotion without enough preparation to do it professionally and effectively.

- *Don't* be unrealistic about timing. It takes months to read, accept and ready a book for publication.

DOS

- *Do* find out what a publishing house has already brought out, before you send them your magnum opus.

- *Do* present your material properly.

- *Do* read your contract thoroughly.

- *Do* take advice on it.

- *Do* keep writing—your next book should be well underway before your first book hits the bestseller lists.

Chapter 8

Getting it Onstage and Onscreen

Every time a friend succeeds, I die a little.

Gore Vidal

- I have this great idea for a novel. What are my chances of having a movie made of it?

- Some of the things you see in the theatre these days aren't worth staging. I'm sure I could write a play.

- If you write a play, can you make sure the actors say exactly the lines you wrote?

- Let's say I wrote a play and the audience liked it but the critics didn't. Would it run?

- Are television plays more difficult to write than stage plays?

Take one would-be writer who doesn't go to the theatre very often, preferably one who thinks that George Bernard Shaw and Terence Rattigan were the last worthwhile dramatists. Fill up the would-be playwright's bookshelves with musty copies of J. B. Priestley and Lennox Robinson, and his mind with some well-worn theme like the plight of the widowed mother left to live out her days with the self-absorbed, materially orientated younger generation. Give the writer a tin ear, so that he pays no attention to the way real people talk, a typewriter ribbon several hundred years old and a sheaf of near-tissue paper. Make sure the typewriter uses only single spacing. Submit the result to the National Theatre and when it is rejected refuse to acknowledge that there is anything wrong with it. Sure haven't they missed out on genius before?

That is the recipe for the creation of an unsuccessful playwright. The recipe for a successful playwright is more difficult to come by. All the theatre managers agree, however, that there are a few key things every playwright needs to have before he can hope to produce a piece of theatre that will work. The most obvious is knowledge of the theatre. Writers should go to plays often, in order to attune their minds to what modern theatre is about, and also to learn what is theatrically possible and what is not.

Going regularly to the theatre will give some insight into the kind of work favoured by particular managements, although this is not a simple matter of "They produce X kind of play, so I must write an X play." They may be running an apparently endless series of scruffy comedies because there is nothing else being supplied to them, but it is also possible that they find scruffy comedies fill the seats. Viewing from the outside, it is often difficult to make an accurate guess at the real reason.

At all events, a general picture of current trends is all you need. Slavishly tailoring a play for a particular theatre or director is damaging, according to Hugh Leonard, one of Ireland's most successful playwrights, whose work has appeared on television channels around the world and on Broadway with enormous success.

"It's fatal to gear a play to an audience, theatre or director," he maintains. "If you do it, you're bound to write a very bad play."

Leonard also says that there is a lot of truth remaining in a remark made long years ago by Lennox Robinson, one of the people who contributed to the substantial track record of Ireland's Abbey Theatre. Robinson once remarked that when he had a new play submitted to him, he would flip the pages quickly. If he could see that the speeches were all roughly the same length, he knew it would be a bad play, because it was so clearly written chunk after chunk after chunk by someone who never listened to the speech patterns of real people.

Listening and imagination are the essentials of good dialogue writing. Listening is what gives you the flavour of the way your characters should talk, so that they all don't sound like sawn-off versions of yourself. And imagining what those words would sound like, spoken by an actor is vital. An amazing number of writers will happily write paragraphs which look well on paper but which would defy the most intelligent actor to speak in public. This happens because they cannot make the imaginative leap from their typewriter to the stage; because they cannot imaging what an actor would feel like saying those words.

It would seem that would-be playwrights are either the most easily defeated or the most arrogant writers around, if the people at the receiving end of submitted plays are to be believed. Most playwrights receive their rejection slips with total silence. They do not ask for clarification or the reasons for the rejection, or for hints for making it better. They either consign it to a dustbin or shove it in a fresh envelope and post it off to another management. If they do ask to see the play editor or the management of the theatre that rejected their offering, then it is usually a last-ditch effort to change official minds, not an attempt to gain insight into the faults of the work itself.

Hugh Leonard says:

> They just don't buy the rejection. If the author asks to see you, nine times out of ten he is really trying to convince you that it's a great play. He comes to the meeting thinking 'This is a good play, I've still got faith in it,' and you're deadlocked. If you can get a fellow to say 'yes, my play's bad and I know why,' then you've got a playwright there because he will then rewrite. Someone said, and there's a lot of truth in it, that plays are not written— they're re-written.

Director Joe Dowling agrees with Leonard.

When sending back a play, I've always added a line to the effect that if the writer wanted some comments on his or her work, they should contact me. Most didn't bother, I don't know why. Either they thought the thing was brilliant, and sent it on straight away to another management, which was fair enough, or they just didn't want to think about it again.

If you are unfortunate enough to have your play rejected, it is wise and professional to ask why. Even if, having seen the comments, you decide that producer/script-editor is wrong about it, the exercise will have given you an insight into their thinking.

Many of the rejection slips which go out to Irish writers every year from theatrical managements find their way into the post because the play submitted was banal, not suitable for production, had unspeakable dialogue, was the product of too many hours spent watching American canned TV programmes, or was cliched melodrama. According to Joe Dowling, too few writers look into the reality of relationships they know when they are seeking material for plays:

> There just aren't enough people writing today who handle everyday problems that are relevant to real people. I'm not saying that a play can't have an isolated approach. What I am saying is that the central theme must be something which makes sense to the people who, hopefully, will come along and watch it, and not just makes sense to them, but move them as well.

The other fault which frequently crops up is poor presentation. Theatre people at the receiving end of plays will read almost anything. They will go through handwritten dialogue on miserable paper that looks as if it's been whirling around in a washing machine for a week. But they do not have to like it, and they would have to be saints if a desire didn't arise in them to skip bits here and there and to shorten their misery. Generally, they do not skip, but it is simple courtesy to present them with clean typescript in which the characters are clearly delineated, the divisions between their speeches made clear, and the stage directions easy to understand.

How long your play will remain under consideration by any given management varies. Some readers get through a manuscript quickly, some do not. If you are a well-known writer, you will get a decision more quickly than a novice. Assuming a theatrical management likes the look of your play, the work is not over. They may ask you to make changes. You will also want to look at the cast list. Many managements talk of the writer having a "reasonable" approval of the cast. This is an "how long is a piece of string" conception; after all, how reasonable is "reasonable"? It is not, however, usually a major source of contention.

Occasionally a writer will have a particular actor in mind for a given part, and may feel a little cheated if that actor is very popular and therefore unavailable, but a compromise is usually acceptable to both parties. After that, the major question is— how many of the rehearsals should you attend? Opinions vary. Some people say that the writer should go along to the first reading, to explain any obscurities and listen for obvious flaws which call for re-writing. The writer who attends the initial rehearsal also needs to check the text. A mistake which is plausible and neatly typed may not be spotted by a director, and an actor will happily learn the line. One playwright had a line referring to "beggars" which the typist and actor rendered as "buggers" and which everybody accepted as valid within the play's context until quite late in the day when the writer attended a rehearsal and spotted the bloomer. The word skewed the direction of the scene, and the problem about it having been spotted so late in the rehearsal cycle was that, under pressure, the actor tended to revert to what he had originally learned.

Whether, having attended that initial rehearsal, you should then be a regular presence in the theatre until the opening night is a matter of opinion. Some theatre people feel that the writer is as well to be away from the theatre during that period, not worrying the thing like a bone and disturbing himself with thoughts that perhaps the actors won't learn the text in time, but returning in the final week when the production is in reasonably good shape to offer any extra help he can. On the other hand, there is the body of opinion which holds that, if the playwright is minded to be civil and helpful, the director and cast can only benefit by having him around all the time.

"If the writer knows where his function begins and ends, then he's a great addition to rehearsals," one director told me. "If he doesn't, then he is at best an obstacle and at worst an intolerable bloody nuisance."

Writing for the big screen is a dream to which many novelists would be ashamed to admit. The bright lights. The glamour. The stars. The locations. The money.

It all adds up. Yet, if you read writers' biographies and autobiographies (and you should—the bad experiences which have happened to the great figures of literature make one's own set-backs seem minor and even, on occasion, well-deserved) then you will find writer after writer coming a cropper on the Hollywood sign.

Sagas have been written about the trek westward in the thirties and forties of some of America's major literary figures, lured by massive contracts, by promises of editorial freedom and by the excitement of contributing to a medium only then coming into its own. F. Scott Fitzgerald, Robert Benchley, Dorothy Parker and even Faulkner. They all went. They all took the dollars and the temptations—mostly alcoholic—that went with them. They protected themselves from self-contempt and the contempt of others by chemical intervention and personal parody; at one stage, according to apocrypha, Dorothy Parker was seen leaning out of the window of her first-floor writer's garret, yelling "Let me out of here—I'm as sane as you are!"

Two blunt pieces of advice.

- Don't write your novel with a partly hidden agenda that you will eventually have it made into a film.

- If someone from the world of film expresses an interest in an option on your material, take advice, take the money and take six grains of salt along with every promise made.

Film people tend to see writers as a necessary evil. Increasingly, directors see them as not even necessary, taking cameras out on the road and developing scripts themselves on an ad hoc basis.

Although there has been a breakup of the great production monoliths of old, and despite the fact that smaller, independent or satellite production studios are opening in every country where such developments are tax-wise options, there is still no immediate, straightforward or simple way into movie-making. The best and most recent book for any would-be screenwriter to learn from is William Goldman's *Adventures in the Screen Trade*. Goldman is a prolific and powerful novelist and a hugely successful screenwriter, responsible, *inter alia*, for *Butch Cassidy and the Sundance Kid* and *The Princess Bride*.

Read him about handling your own or someone else's work for the screen. Read him about seeing your own work man-handled by a "professional screenwriter." Read him about the process whereby a project which one week is a certain block-buster success which will see people queuing in the street overnight for a viewing, the following week is a non-starter, the producers of which are suddenly unreachable and uninterested. Read him to be depressed and amused by the whole tatty, tinselly, fascinating business of writing for film.

Writing for television can be much the same process on the smaller scale and nearer home. Useful in giving you the ground rules is a helpful note produced by Ireland's RTE Television which will be sent to you on request. It says:

> Ignore camera angles. Write the action as you see it. Do not have too many characters involved in the same scene. Keep the scenes as short as is consistent with the action you wish to portray. In other words, when you have made your point, told the part of the story the scene represents, end the scene. It is not intended to impose limits on the number of characters in your play, but bear in mind that plays are strictly budgeted and actors must be paid. Limit the number of characters to

those essential to your plot.

> Dialogue should sound the way people speak, and through
> dialogue (and action) you will delineate your character. But
> do not reproduce every word. This is dramatic writing and re-
> member the secret here, as in all art, is in selection.

Many television stations produce guidebooks or pamphlets
defining their overall style or the specifics of an individual
programme. This is true even of departments like Religion,
where, if you want to provide the "Thought for the Day" item,
you will find the Religious Department are likely to have an
informative page that they will mail to you on request, giving
their script specifications.

> "Writing for television is extremely competitive, and the
> standard of acceptance is therefore very high," says the Beeb,
> in its handbook entitled *Writing for the BBC*. "Most of the
> regular contributors are professional freelance writers who
> contribute to all the media, but tend to give the major part of
> their effort to television. The new writer is nevertheless
> welcomed, even though the opportunities are relatively
> limited."

Or, put it another way, we've got this welcome mat, but it's
just a touch crowded. It was crowded yesterday. It is crowded
today. It will be crowded tomorrow. If you want to join the
jostling crowd on that welcome mat (which is not specific to the
Beeb—all major television networks that include drama in their
offerings have it) then there are a number of questions you need
to ask yourself.

Can I think in pictures?

Television stations, every day of the week, get scripts which
address major philosophical issues and in which words dance,
shimmer and collude to marvellous effect. The only problem is
that there are no pictures. No context. No location. No visual
development of the story. No motifs. No visible expressions.
No sense of space or time or colour. Those scripts tend to

bounce back. If there is a decent, positive, supportive script editor at the initial receiving end, that editor may put in a note suggesting that the writer might be well advised to try a radio station with what is essentially a radio play. When you have an idea for a media play, you need to be clear that it requires to be seen as well as heard—and that it can *justify* being seen as well as heard.

Can I show, not tell?

You have seen them, haven't you? The TV plays where two characters sit on a couch and tell each other about what's happening in the relationships next door. You, in the audience, want to tell them to shut up and let us see what's going on in the neighbouring house. They are telling us, not showing us. Aha, I hear you say. But didn't Shakespeare have these great chunks of scenes where pages and soldiers and door-opening janitors told the audience or each other the story so far, introduced all the characters and speculated about where the action would go next? Sure, he did. Of course he did. Certainly. Indubitably. Dammit, he *had* to. He had no scenery, no women, no lights, no special effects, no filming on location, no authentic props. He had actors and words and that was it. Inevitably, he had to use both to set the scene and paint the background against which ensuing action might be understood. That is no excuse for modern-day playwrights whether they are scripting for the live theatre or for television. In radio, there may have to be a certain amount of scene-setting, but exchange of historical information between actors should always be regarded as the least acceptable option.

Can I make the most of actors' talents?

The actor is handed his script, and the description of his non-speaking opening scene goes something like this:

> Slow mix from exterior reveals Michael, alone in the seaside shelter. He is in denim, and is reading a document. As we watch, he crumples it and throws it away, then retrieves it and holds it in his hands as the camera moves into a big close

up on his face. We see him remembering his days in the IRA, and reflecting on how the first idealistic optimism turned into a brutal repetition of violence for the sake of violence, gradually eroding his sense of self and his ambitions for the future. Can he, at this stage, break loose from the IRA and set up a new life for himself elsewhere, perhaps Australia?

The actor, assuming he has brought his brains to the party, is likely at this point to cry halt:

Hold it just one tiny second here. The viewer doesn't know who this guy is. I'm sitting there with this lump of paper and I'm to tell the viewers all about the IRA and my lifestory and Australia—without *words*? Just by *expressions*? You wouldn't, by any chance, like me to convey the contents of the telephone directory to the camera by telepathy?"

Be reasonable. Actors can do a lot, and if it is clear to them what is going on, they can do a great deal without words. No script should put too many words into an actor's mouth. But, contrariwise, no script should put an intolerable burden on an actor's ESP or on his facial expressions.

Can I keep to the point?
TV time is costly. TV viewers are fickle, not to say inattentive, mentally lazy, and gifted with attention spans provided from God's discount store. You therefore cannot afford, in script terms, to sod about digressing and diversifying when they want to know where the plot is going and what's going to happen next. Little scenes with irrelevant characters being picturesque should be cut, and every line in the play should be subjected to the question "Does this scene move the action on? Does it help us get to the point?"

Can I write dialogue that is authenthic and varied?
People should speak like they would sound in the real world. Obvious? Easy? Uh, uh. Someone brought me a videotape production presenting the corporate worth of a leading pharmaceutical company, in which there was a scene showing a

sick seven-year-old in bed. The child's father advanced into view. The child looked up.

"Oh, father," said the child. "I am ill."

I rewound the tape in the hope that I might have imagined it. No, it happened again.

"Oh, father," said the child. "I am ill."

At the time, I had a partly domesticated seven year old of my own, and he had never said to me Oh, mother, he was ill. He yelled words to the effect that Ma, he was dying. He came in and leaned up against walls and allowed that his head was splitting and his chest was sore. He occasionally came in covered in blood and tears (he tended to be low on sweat) and wept an incoherence at me. But "Oh, Father...?" Oh, Mother!

If you are going to write the words people speak in real life, you have to pay attention to the way they speak them in real life. The phrases that are current. The sentence structures. The images. The slang. In addition, one person should not sound like another person. Your secretary does not sound like your golfing buddy. Your mother does not talk the same way as your international VIP does. The writing of dialogue should never be approached as if the central task was the exposition of data. What people say is important. But they way in which they say it is a valuable input to the characters being created and the backgrounds being evoked.

Can I shut up my characters?
They have to do more than talk. A glance, a silence or a strangled dither can say much more than a well-crafted sentence, if they happen in the right place. When you are writing for drama, you have to see the characters in front of you, and take messages from their body language and from their silences just as clearly as you take messages from the words they utter.

Can I identify with each of my characters in sequence?
Good drama is about conflict of some kind. Therefore you must have characters at odds with one another. When this happens, it is all too easy to create a good guy and a bad guy. It is much

better drama if you have a good guy with bits of bad in him and a bad guy with bits of good in him. That way your audience is not divided into camps favouring stereotypes. The only way to create truly human characters with all of the well-rounded complexity which that implies, is to identify with each of them in turn, so that what action any one of them takes is totally credible and of interesting confusion to the audience.

Can I tell a story?
Stand up and tell the story of the play you plan to write to whoever lives with you. If you can't tell it inside two minutes so that they get the central gist, then there is something wrong with your yarn.

Can I keep critics out of my mind?
If you have a picture in the back of your mind of glowering beetle-browed critics waiting to tell the world that you cannot write and that you are not good enough to call yourself a playwright, then you should stop right now. Imagine the audience and concentrate on keeping them enthralled.

Can I talk to other people about my play while I'm writing it?
You can. But you should not. Some of the more quality conscious American multi-nationals give their managers little cards to stick in their breast pockets to remind them to perform a number of forgettable tasks during each working day.

I am convinced that most writers should have a card to put in their breast pocket, which reads "Shut up and write!" Whether it's drama or novels or short stories, people talk too much about their writing and write too little. Great novels have been dissipated over dinner tables and in smoky pubs. There is a great danger that, having articulated a story to a third party, the imperative of writing it becomes less urgent. If the person who hears it responds apathetically or with hostility, there is even less incentive to take pen in hand. My personal confidence in on-going writers' workshops is, accordingly, somewhat limited, because of the amount of sharing of plot and character and extracts that goes on during such workshops. Writers should write. Not talk. Writers should allow themselves to talk about a book or a play only when they have the thing finished. Otherwise, they are effectively living on credit to which they are not entitled.

Say if I cannot write a full length play?

So what? Write a one-act play. Somewhere between fifteen minutes and forty five in length, a good tight dramatic incident and a small cast of characters. Work up to the major league stuff.

Is it OK to write speeches?

You want a straight answer? No, it is not OK to write speeches. In the past, when plays were written about kings and queens and statesmen, the odd speech was acceptable, even predictable. If a guy like a king is out there giving speeches to the swarming masses all day, we kind of expect him to let loose a few speeches over the tea table, too. When you have a cast of three working class men down a sewer hammering away at a dislocated rivet, speeches are not on. Keep it short, to the point and interactive.

Can I keep a secret?

No good play is written by someone who puts out all of the elements at one go and then plays around with them. Secrets have to be kept. Think about it. Most of the great plays, whether they are comedies, tragedies or musicals, have a secret which is kept throughout the night's entertainment. So, with *Who's Afraid of Virginia Woolf*? you have a secret about the existence or non-existence of a child. In *The Importance of Being Earnest,* you have concealment of the central character's identity. In *Waiting for Godot,* to the end the secret of who he is and when he is going to arrive is kept. In *A Chorus Line*, we do not know throughout the bulk of the action who will be finally chosen and who rejected.

Should I pose a question?

The earlier the better, and keep the question unanswered as long as you possibly can. The question in *Death of a Salesman* is about how badly Willie Loman is doing and what disaster is going to happen to him. The question in *A Doll's House* is how this wife is going to cope with her (apparent) inadequacies. The question in *Klute* is twofold: will the murderer be caught and will this prostitute and this detective fall in love?

Will I be able to build up tension?

You have to. Not to explosion point. Just to the point where a sudden extra element throws everybody. Have a look at Neil Simon's *The Odd Couple*. Tension is built, Felix arrives in with his burnt culinary offering, and all hell breaks loose. Tension comes from conflict, spoken or hinted at, and conflict is central to a play. It may be possible to write a play about pleasant people getting along pleasantly in a pleasant setting without saying unpleasant things to each other, but hell, I don't want to have tickets for an opening night of sweetness and understanding. Me, I want gossip, bad mouthing, dishonesty, disloyalty, venom and hatred. Or in Alice Roosevelt Longworth's great comment, "If you can't say anything good about anybody, sit right here by me."

The main dos and don'ts of writing drama, whether for radio, TV, film or the stage, are these:

DON'T

- *Don't* use the characters as your mouthpiece. If they all sound like you, no matter how witty you are it becomes tedious.

- *Don't* think in terms of words alone. Drama is about sounds and sights and expressions as well as telling ripostes.

- *Don't* turn out sausage machine characters. Differentiate them, not just by sex or superficialities, but by the way they think. Write down their letters and thoughts and private habits, even if these never appear in the finished work.

- *Don't* bore people. Imagine that your audience is always on the verge of leaving, and prevent that. Every five minutes, giving them a reason for staying.

- *Don't* add irrelevancies.

DOS

- *Do* allow your characters to talk the way they really would—pauses and slang and all.

- *Do* create conflict.

- *Do* deal in emotions.

- *Do* reveal things layer by layer, onion-fashion.

- *Do* visualise what you are doing at all times. When you are writing a radio play, close your eyes and imagine how much reality can be conjured up by your words and some special effects.

Chapter 9

Writing for the Spoken Word: Radio and TV

Is this the Party to whom I am speaking?

Lily Tomalin as Ernestine The Operator

- I have often wondered if the guy on the morning radio programme makes it up as he goes along, or if someone scripts it for him?

- How can I get to read short inputs on local radio?

- Where do documentaries get their scriptwriters?

- Is writing for TV or radio much different to writing for newspapers?

- Is there much of a market for radio and TV scriptwriters?

Quite apart from drama, which has been dealt with in the previous chapter, radio and television present an enormous potential market for freelance writers, yet relatively few freelances think first of radio or television as a market. There are so many reasons for this. First of all, many would-be writers don't appreciate just how much of any transmission is scripted. They assume that each presenter just naturally spouts reams of prose. In some cases, of course, they do, but most programmes have scripted elements in them, even though these, due to the skills of the presenters, are not readily apparent. One of the most successful writers in the freelance radio field here simply guessed her way into the field.

"I was just listening to an item on a programme one day, and I suddenly realised that someone had written it," she told me. "I felt I could write the same kind of thing better. I did, and they accepted it and wanted more."

The second problem is that writing something you hope to see on a printed page and something you hope to hear on the air are quite different tasks requiring quite different skills.

"A great many writers don't seem to be able to see the difference between writing for radio and writing for, say, a newspaper," says a radio producer who has been in the business for twenty years. "People send me things which would be fine in a paper—all nice sentences with beginnings and middles and ends and good, well-chosen words and logically laid out points, and they simply won't work in radio. Writing for radio needs to be less formal, more the way ordinary people talk, not carefully rounded sentences that look well on a page. It's how it sounds that counts."

With the exception of a few programmes on radio which use what are essentially written essays, or extremely formal linking scripts. "How it sounds" is the most important single guiding principle an aspiring radio writer can use. This applies equally to TV, where words are in partnership or even subordinate to pictures, and closely argued essays are useless.

The best writing for radio often looks awful in print. Thankfully very few people, outside of the writer, the producer, and the presenter have to see it, and as all three are in the business of putting spoken words out on the airwaves, they do not care how the words look on paper. A couple of years back, I had prepared a script for one of the best readers of the spoken word alive and broadcasting today. He is one of those magicians who can make three pages of closely typed script sound like wild improvisation off the top of his hard-working head. The script was tailored as precisely as I could make it to his personal style. Which meant that there were pet slang phrases in it, little exclamations, short stretches where he moved from the central point to a favourite theme, and even a couple of points where he could seem to be collecting his thoughts before giving a huge swatch of technical information. For various reasons, the script had to be vetted by the radio station's resident lawyer. He ploughed through it with a growing look of distaste and finally held the pages up by one corner.

"Is this some kind of draft?" he asked plaintively. "It's dreadful, you know. Full of half-sentences and slang. I'd hate for anybody outside of the organisation to see this." In due course, the awful script was broadcast, sounded super and was never identified as a script by the listeners, which was the purpose of the exercise. Luckily, this Upstairs man had a watching brief only on the legalities. In an organisation where he had wider powers, the script would have been rewritten to sound like a piece of budding legislation, and the listeners would have switched channels.

The other point my Man Upstairs picked up was that there was repetition in the script. He painstakingly indicated where thought (a) had been covered again, in different words, in paragraph sixteen. As it should have been. People reading a newspaper article or a section of a book can stop at what they see as the obviously important places and re-read them. Or, the sub-editor may decide to help that process along by putting the vital material in a different type face, to attract and hold the reader's interest. In radio, and from a platform, you cannot do that, short of (in platform speeches) turning your back on the audience entirely and writing the key points on a blackboard, which reduces the audience to resentful schoolchildren. So repetition is important. Not literal repetition. People will not hold still for a chorus of the same thoughts in the same words. But a re-cap, using different illustrations, will help the listener not to miss out on something which is significant.

On this point, the BBC's briefs for radio reporters always stress the need to write the way people speak, as opposed to the way people would like to think that they speak:

When you write a radio report, the language must be plain.

Sentence structure should be simple. Simple subject. Simple predicate. No compound sentences. A participle phrase has no place in a radio report. Prepositional phrases should be rare. Subordinate, appositional and all such clauses you do not need. Words must be simple words. Don't hunt for synonyms. Synonyms escalate misunderstanding. A ship is a ship. A boat is a boat. Not a vessel or craft. Just use the same word over again. It reinforces listener comprehension. It'll sound OK.

The most important concepts can be thus expressed. F.D. Roosevelt's speechwriter once wrote

"We are endeavouring to construct a more inclusive society."

Roosevelt promptly changed it so that it read:

"We're going to make a country in which no one is left out."

Real words. Contractions ("We're," rather than "We are.") Reference to individuals. Strong verbs.

First degree words are important when you are writing for radio and television. First degree words are the ones which immediately bring an image to mind. Others must be "translated" through the first degree words before you see the image. Those are second/third degree words. First degree words are usually more precise, too.

First degree words	Second or third degree
Face	Visage, countenance
Book	Volume, tome
Stay	Abide, remain, reside

When you are writing a script for somebody to read on the air, you must edit out redundancies. The way Reader's Digest handle their condensing process is a classic example of how to do this. Here's an example:

Version One

Have you ever wondered how banks rate you as a credit risk? You know, of course, that it's some combination of facts about your income, your job and so on. But actually, many banks have a scoring system...

Version Two

Have you ever wondered how banks rate you as a credit risk? Many banks have a scoring system…

Remember, when you write for broadcast, that people listening or viewing cannot revise or put what you say in context. If, in order to understand what you are talking about, they have to make mental reference to something else, their mind becomes detached from your presentation for the duration, and you may, ultimately, lose them completely. Kit out your facts and statistics in examples, stories, analogies and pictures, or else they will not work efficiently for you on the airwaves.

Radio and television hate windy phrases like:

"At the present time" when you can say "now."

"In the event of" when you can say "if."

"In the majority of instances" when you can say "usually."

"The door which you see beside me," when you can say "The door I'm standing beside."

Windy phrases must go from a radio or television script. So, too, must passive verbs.

"The headquarters was occupied by seven insurgents."

This is passive and has seven words.

"Seven insurgents held the headquarters."

This has five words and a bit of life in it.

There should be no dithering and unnecessary negatives should go.

"The answer does not rest with carelessness or incompetence. It lies largely in having enough of the appropriate people to do the job."

That should be changed to something more direct, like this:

"The answer is having enough people or the right people to do the job."

Although the approach to a radio or TV script is radically different to the approach used in writing a feature for a newspaper, some of the other rules still apply. Just as it is vital to know the name of the Features Editor in your national newspaper, it is also essential to know what type of radio programme you are writing for and who the correct contact person is. Nothing maddens a producer of a programme specialising in frothy, 2-minute topicalities as much as receiving a piece from a freelance which is tailor-made for a half hour monologue programme. It wastes his time, it insults him as an individual producer doing his best to stamp a different mark on his show, and it indicates that the writer submitting the piece either doesn't listen to radio at all, or is unable to see major differences between various programme types.

The trick is to listen, make sure that what you want to write fits the particular programme, submit it to a producer whose name you have correctly and who is currently in charge of the programme concerned (never send anything to presenters) and follow it up. If the piece is reasonably topical, a telephone reminder will not go amiss. Otherwise, let a few weeks lapse and drop a note or phone the producer.

If you are lucky, you will happen along at the right time. I once provided an average of seventy-five short scripts a week for a daily radio programme. When I moved on to something else, the producer asked me to find him a replacement. I gave him six names. None of them ended up writing for the programme, because none of them a) listened to it and b) listened to the way people talk. They were writers, but not spoken-word writers. There is always a market for good spoken-word writers.

Radio and TV fees vary tremendously. Areas which use a fair amount of non commissioned material (like drama) have scales of payment worked out. Other sections tend to have low payments for non-staffers, simply because they budget for programmes without always planning to use freelance work. In other words, if you worm your way into writing for a well established programme, they are likely to pay you buttons in the beginning. After you have proved yourself invaluable and they have figured a way of fitting you into the accounts, you can battle for more. If you know you're good, and they know you're good, and they can't get anyone to do as good a job cheaper, you will be well paid.

Programme times, titles and producers change so quickly that it would be unhelpful to include a programme-by-programme guide here. Programme guides give details of who produces which programme. Some departments use no freelance work at all, but all departments are worth trying.

Where local radio stations exist, they can provide both a market and a worthwhile testing ground for script ideas. It is not profitable, and there is no continuity, but is it useful for novice radio writers to see, in miniature, the complete working of a radio station, and, in addition, if they are lucky enough to have their offering passed by the local committee, to see what happens to their script as it goes through the broadcasting process. Think short, think fast and think simple.

The dos and don'ts of writing for the spoken word include:

DON'TS
- *Don't* worry about how a script looks.

- *Don't* use passive verbs.

- *Don't* use second degree words.

- *Don't* use subordinate clauses or brackets—they're difficult for a listener to imagine and even more difficult for a presenter to inflect.

- *Don't* use windy phrases.

DOS

- *Do* listen for how your script sounds.

- *Do* listen to radio programmes (and watch TV programmes) so you know which programme requires which material.

- *Do* cut. Briefer is better.

- *Do* write short sentences.

- *Do* write the way your presenter talks.

Chapter 10

Public Relations and Advertising

After I'm dead I'd rather have people ask why I have no monument that why I have one.

Cato the Elder

Many freelance writers take on small public relations accounts. Like the girl with the curl in the middle of her forehead, these can be very very good or horrid.

The horrid clients are the ones who pay a tiny fee for total devotion. They expect a PRO to be a press agent, using her knowledge of journalism and friendship with journalists to get them a daily mention in all the newspapers and on the radio. They also expect her to be a magician, squashing all bad news emanating from their business. Quite a few freelances, wooed by the idea of regular money for which creative writing doesn't have to be done, give in and live up to this expectation, thus muddying the water for everybody else.

The first important thing to realise about public relations is that a PRO is only as good as her management allows her to be. If a firm (or society, or whatever) is closed-in or crooked, or mean, or incompetent, or any combination of these four, the PRO is icing on a dud cake, and will do her own reputation no good at all by fronting for them. Indeed, public relations should never be simply a fronting job. One of the major functions of PR is to alert management to possible public reaction to new policies. To do this, PR people need to be involved in the company at a high enough level to influence policy making.

Sadly, by virtue of their being less than full time at the job, freelances tend not to operate at that level. So they are treated as journalistic syringes; the company puts the information into them and expects them to get it, in turn, into the media. It is possible to make the job work on that basis, but it is important to remember, as a freelance, that your name appears on the press releases, and yours in the voice that journalists hear on the phone, and therefore, if the company is a nasty or ill-organised operation, then no matter how minimal your commitment to them, some of that nastiness or sloppiness will rub off on your image. This does not apply to the full-time PR consultant, who is committed, not to any one company, but to a PR consultancy firm.

Freelance public relations work, could, in theory, be done by anybody with intelligence, a typewriter and some background knowledge, but in practice, it is the preserve of drop-outs from existing PR setups, and of journalists. Most freelance journalists, sooner or later, are offered PR work. It is worthwhile to do it, even for a short time, if only to educate oneself out of the easy contempt many "straight" journalists have for the difficult job a PRO does.

One of the reasons people ask experienced journalists to do PR work for them is because they hope to benefit from an old pals' act. They may talk to you about your expertise, but what they really hope is that you are a personal pal of several journalists and that you will persuade these pals to run regular features on your clients. A key step, therefore, in taking on a PR account is to find out exactly what expectations the client has, and what exactly you are expected to do.

The standard definition of public relations is that it's "the deliberate planned and sustained effort to establish and maintain mutual understanding between an organisation and its public." Remember that though many people automatically do a mental switch whenever they hear the word "public," substituting the word "press," there is in fact a big difference. Getting material into a newspaper is publicity. Making sure that the image of a company or society (or whatever) which the general public holds is a fair and accurate one quite often has little to do with press publicity.

One of the most highly paid full-time public relations officers I know emphasises this aspect of the job above all others. "I see one of my main responsibilities to my clients as ensuring that anything they do, any particularly good service for consumers that they have, doesn't go unnoticed by the consumers. PR in that sense is doing good and getting credit for it," she says.

Find out all you can about the client in advance. Several PR companies make a practice of sending their top executives into the factory or offices of a new client for a week before they begin representing that client. This way, they learn all they can about the operations, products and methods of their client, they get the "feel" of the place and inevitably turn up some of the sensitive areas which may pose PR problems later. This is a good method, if you can spare the time for it, because you will, even in the area of publicity, spot angles for stories which the clients themselves won't notice.

A PR client can be any sort of individual or organisation, ranging from a budding politician to a musical society. From the PRO's point of view, who the client is matters little compared with the much more vital question—"Who is the PR answerable to?" Ideally the short answer is one person, nominated by the management or standing committee or whoever. If the PRO is at the mercy of more than one person, half her time will be wasted answering the phone to people from the society or organisation who have dreamed up some damfool idea for her to do, regardless of the fact that six other people from the same outfit have already rung her that morning with the same damfool idea.

The trick, if you are a PR operating on the outside, is to establish responsibility to one person and that way at least one person will be happy. The other way, nobody is happy.

The day-to-day details of public relations work varies, depending on the outfit. It can encompass writing press releases, drafting letters to the press, organising press conferences and suggesting outlines for speeches for your managing director or head bottle-washer. It should also take in the preparation of a press-cuttings book, in which you log everything which appears in print about your client. This is useful on two counts. It first of all gives you the benefit of neatly organised hindsight, so that you can plan policy for next year, based on what happened this year. But is also is a valuable piece of evidence for your client, indicating what was successful in media terms and what was not.

Where you get the cuttings with which to fill your cuttings book depends on the size and wealth of your client. A large and wealthy one will happily use a press-cuttings service (details in the telephone book) to supply the necessary material. Small and poor clients expect their public relations people to provide a press-cutting and media-monitoring service as part of their work. Providing this entails reading all of the newspapers and magazines in your catchment area with a finer than fine-toothcomb, and developing a "PRO's eye." I know one public relations woman who can spot a reference to one of her clients halfway down a page filled with thousands of words and dozens of other stories.

Monitoring radio is more difficult, if only because radio goes on all day long and is never just a matter of listening to the programme on which you know your client is due to appear. You also need to watch those programmes which may throw up opportunities to be capitalised on by you or your client.

If, example, your client runs a leisure complex, it is not sufficient to listen to sport and leisure programmes. It is also necessary to hear news broadcasts of current affairs programmes and radio chat shows, so that if an opportunity arises for your client to appear, or to respond by letter to a newly raised controversy, you will spot it first. It is vital to hear precisely what was said. Producers do not take kindly to the phone call that begins—"Hey, listen, I heard a bit of your show this morning, and there was a thing on it about hang-gliding— could you tell me what was said?" The best way to obviate the problem is to have one of those radios which has a built-in cassette machine handy to you at all times. That way, the moment an interesting topic is introduced, all you have to do is press a button and you have an instant recording of it. Alternatively, you could ask one of what the Americans call "shut-ins" to do it for you. "Shut-ins" are people who for one reason or another stay at home, and are glad to earn money in situ.

Costing this kind of work is very difficult. There are many organisations to which journalists give public relations consultancy for nothing. It's a regular feature of a reporter's life to be telephoned by another reporter with a "Hi there, I'm doing PR for the XYZ Charity, and I was wondering..." Musical societies and other social groups expect voluntary PR service, usually from a member of the society, and often get excellent work. Which does not help if you are offered a small PR job, and you do not know how to charge. The rule of thumb is—charge more than you think you should, because there will be more work involved than you ever imagined. Decide how much time—a day, two days a week, you want to devote to it, and cost accordingly. For writers, this is often difficult. But if you work that out, according to your speed of writing, you could turn out two one thousand word articles for a particular market in a day, thus earning £40, then for one day's PR work you could charge roughly that.

Writing for PR firms is another market which is worth considering. PR firms rarely have specialists on staff, although they quite often have clients who require written specialist material. The important thing is that you have an area of specialised knowledge. If, say, you know all there is to be known about (a) gardening, and (b) trains, it is a very good idea to set out your qualifications in these areas and sent them to all the public relations firms (you'll find them listed in the Communications' Directory) indicating your willingness to write on those topics. This is a sprat which quite often lands a biggish fish.

It is considerably more difficult to get into advertising on a freelance basis. There are very few writers working as freelances in the ad business, and most of those who are, happen to be freelances only because they have spent years in various agencies, and have decided that staffing does not suit them. Starting the other way around—trying to set up as an advertising copy writer without first working in an agency, seems to be unheard of, although there's no law that says you can't do it that way.

Ad agencies do not like to farm writing work out, if they can avoid it. The ad world is a gossipy one, and for Agency A to be parcelling out its work to freelances would quickly establish it as lacking its own creative staff. Again, there is a problem of confidentiality. If Agency A has a client in the food processing business who has just come up with a way to take all the calories out of butter, and wants an ad campaign built around that, he might feel a little uneasy at the thought of all of his technical secrets being packages for taking home like a single of chips.

Nevertheless, there are freelances in the business who survive, as do freelances everywhere else in the writing business, by being efficient, discreet, sober when called upon, and creative. How do you get an agency to sit up and take notice of the fact that you are all of these things? "By hawking yourself around," one managing director of an advertising agency in Dublin says. "Just make up a portfolio, damn someone's soul until he agrees to see you, show him your stuff and follow it up. And even then, there's a seventy per cent chance he'll never use you."

Making up a portfolio is relatively easy if you have worked in the business prior to going out on your own. If you start on your own, it's not so simple. The advice would seem to be: get hold of an artist/photographer, work out a few ideas for possible ads with him, do up a snazzy version of several and the go sell yourself and your portfolio. The getting together with an artist or photographer would seem to be a good idea anyway, as agencies appear to be more willing to contract work out to what they view as a coherent freelance service, rather than a scattered hack.

Chapter 11

Growing Markets

Lack of money is the root of all evil.

George Bernard Shaw

- You write because of inspiration, not because there is a market for it, right?

- How can you find out about specialist markets?

- Anybody can write romance novels, can't they?

- How can I look credible when I'm seeking to do specialist writing?

- I was thinking of writing something to be published on audio cassette. Is there a market there?

The first of these questions is the crucial one. If you can only write in response to the descent of the Muse upon your shoulder, and if making a living is a minor consideration for you, then this chapter will be of little relevance to you.

But if you're still with me, let me tell you a story. Or three.

The first story is about a woman who had done "a bit of writing" for many years. She had never made much money at it, but she liked to see her by-line in the papers and she got on well with editors. Although she made relatively little money, she had become a member of the NUJ by virtue of the fact that this money was her only source of income. It was a meeting of her branch of the NUJ which jolted her into action. At this particular meeting, those present addressed the application for membership of a woman moving away from an earlier career, who had now decided she wanted to do freelance writing. The trade union had asked the applicant to state how much she was earning, annually, by writing. She had also been asked to bring supportive evidence to prove her claim, this being one of the steps the union takes to ensure that people accepted for membership are capable of supporting themselves.

The applicant stated that she was earning £26,000 a year. The writer who was already a member of the union watched dumbly, as members of the NUJ queried the figure until eventually its accuracy was proven to their satisfaction.

"Satisfaction" is perhaps an inappropriate word, since most of those present earned considerably less than £26,000, and the arrival of an affluent newcomer undoubtedly engendered mixed feelings.

"I went home that night," the by-line-relisher told me later, and I worked out that on average, I was earning £7,000 a year from writing. I decided that I had at least as much talent as that new applicant, and that instead of earning "pin money" I could earn a very good living, give my family the security one income couldn't provide, and the holidays we've always thought were beyond our means.

The writer took a week off actual writing to assess her strengths and see where they matched emerging markets. She got cheeky and rang people for advice.

"I want to make a living at writing," she told them. "Can you tell me about markets I may be missing?"

A journalist friend told her about an forthcoming conference that needed a rapporteur and that would also, in the coming months, need someone to edit a book based on the conference proceedings. An editor told her of a routine task that would pay a regular fee for a half day's commitment per week. A PR agency commissioned her to write anonymous features for distribution by the agency to provincial newspapers, who used them, free of charge, on behalf of their client. At the end of the week, the writer, without becoming more visible, in the sense of producing a block-buster bestseller, had, nonetheless, almost doubled the income she stood to make that year. She had done it by shaking off her own passivity and by exploring markets she had never examined up to that point.

"The curious thing is that I did almost *no* selling," she told me. "Just indicating that I was interested in doing more work seemed to open doors for me."

The second story to be told is that of Derek, although that is not his real name. Derek is one of my favourite people. He is also one of the most productive lazy people I have ever met. His career has been motivated by laziness, his activity fuelled only by his desire to buy leisure time.

One of David's more interesting current commissions is to produce a non-fiction book on a topical and controversial subject. The publisher had floated the idea past several writers whom were flattered, but who marinaded the flattery over a considerable period of time. When the publisher floated the same idea past Derek he was taken aback to receive, twenty four hours later, a summary of what Derek felt the book should deal with, an indication of the research which would be required, an estimate of the time needed to do both research and writing, and based on all of the foregoing, a suggested advance figure. The publisher read the three-page document and telephoned Derek.

"You don't beat around the bush, do you?"

"No."

"I had hoped to bring this thing out three months from now, because it's so current. I'm afraid it will go off the boil if I let it take as long as the plan you outline would need."

"In that case, in addition to the advance, give me a research fee—a straight fee, not part of the royalties. Make it about two thousand pounds and I'll be able to free myself from everything else for the time it'll take."

"Two thousand. You've got to be kidding!"

Derek didn't bother to answer that, and the publisher said he would get back to him. He did. Derek is now half-way through the research for a book which will sell, not because of his name, but because it will be the right book at the right time.

This chapter's third story concerns a man who escaped.

John escaped from a Good Job. He was a sub-editor on a solid, respectable newspaper in London. Regular hours. Good money. No major threats in his future, and the most recent challenge in his past was the task of coming to terms with a relatively friendly computer. Coming up to his fortieth birthday, John suddenly became aware of an overwhelming sense of panic. Quiet panic. He realised that he would always be good at his job, but that the dread he now had of getting up in the morning was likely to get worse, rather than better, with time. He could see himself becoming the pillar of society, everybody's best friend, the office mainstay, the father figure to the troubled, and an anecdotal old fool. With the delighted, if startled connivance of his wife, he abandoned the permanent and pensionable job, returned to his home town and set himself up as a freelance. Within weeks, he stumbled upon a factor nobody had ever told him would be important to successful freelancing.

"Marketing by Wandering About," he calls it, in parody of the concept developed by the co-authors in the "*In Search of Excellence*" books.

"I do the editorial and the pictures," he says. "I lay the whole thing out. They get the ads. Each supplement sells the advertisers for the next supplement and some of the papers do extra print runs of particular supplements because advertisers like to have them as giveaways at exhibitions and trade fairs."

Happening on this lucrative growing market did not distract John from the important marketing lesson implicit in his good fortune: that visibility counts.

"I still walk through that open-plan office very purposefully about once a week, even though I often have no express purpose to justify my being there. Every time I do, someone spots me and that John, the-very-man syndrome happens all over again. If people don't see you around, they assume you have emigrated or that you've withdrawn to your study to turn out a massive tome and that you won't want to be disturbed."

What each of the three people have discovered is a growing market. There are many others. Let's look at just a handful of them.

Romance

Although more women today are self-supporting, more of them are also reading romantic novels. The market has been estimated at 24 million regular readers, most of them female.

This side of the Atlantic, the market leader in Romances is Mills & Boon, who are always seeking new writers to produce books between 50,000 and 60,000 words in length, concerned with the development of love between a woman in her teens or twenties and a man in his late twenties or thirties. Exotic locations are preferred and a happy ending is a *sine qua non*.

In common with many other romantic publishing houses, Mills & Boon have an information sheet they will send, free of charge, to aspiring authors who mail them a stamped, self-addressed envelope. Not only do they make their specifications clear to aspirants; they also engage in publicity (including competitions on popular radio programmes) designed to stimulate sales and writers in one fell swoop. Mills & Boon receive close to 4,000 manuscripts every year. Out of those submissions, perhaps twelve, from totally new writers, will be selected for publication. Twelve letters of acceptance. Three thousand nine hundred and eighty-eight rejection slips. Why the imbalance?

One of the reasons is that people think the task is simple. They copy on to the formula common to several romances they may have read, and set out to produce the same sequence of notes in the key melodies of a few chart-toppers, assuming that their inclusion in a new song will ensure a gold disc if not a platinum. It ain't necessarily so.

Because there is existing formula extant does not mean that everybody capable of writing grammatical sentences within that formula will emerge from the exercise with a publishable book. Value of some kind must be added. All of the romance publishers stress that although the central romantic themes are predictable, successful romantic writers are never those who are in the business of churning out the mixture as before. Dolly Parton once remarked of her own appearance that "It costs a lot of money to look this cheap." In similar vein, it requires a lot of effort, inspiration and skill to stay within guidelines while concealing from the reader the existence of those guidelines.

The one writer who is almost certain to fall in the romance stakes is the one who is "slumming" in the *genre*. This is the writer with established competence or unfounded notions of competence in a classier area of literature. Hell, this writer thinks, I'll just toss off a quick bodice-ripper. I mean, boy (maybe in a powdered wig, ruffles at the throat, whip slapping absently at the thigh) meets girl (burgeoning bosom, hooped skirt, fan at the ready and easy on the face patches) boy loses girl (to aged but plausible roue, don't forget the snuff box) boy wins girl again (maybe after a little swordplay). Anybody can do that. Beneath me, of course, but what a larf. And anyway, I'll write the thing under some made-up name like Sylvia Filligree or Anthea Raven, so nobody will ever know it's me. I won't have to be ashamed when I'm hugely successful in this grotty writer's cul de sac.

The reality is that very few of the "real" writers who try slumming it in Romance make a success of the venture. Their manuscripts have giveaways in them. Little references go in to preserve the writer's self-respect. The author tries to operate at two levels so that he can continue to believe in his "true" vocation. Or, worst of all, the romance lacks any of the real storyteller's zest, because the writer is so ashamed of what he is doing that he is writing the book the way an uncommitted actor plays a part; he is "doing a walk through."

Technical writing
It's silicon chips with everything, these days. There are massive corporations and tiny "skunkworks" everywhere, trying to develop smaller and better technology to gather, store,

regurgitate and manipulate data of all kinds.

This technology is developed by software and hardware experts who are at one removed from the rest of us on even their good days (if you don't believe me, read the biographies of some of the high-tech pioneers), and who speak English only when they need to in order to order hamburgers or call a cab. The engineers who come up with the new solutions speak a language that the strangers do not know, and this causes major problems when it comes to selling the technology to Joe and Jo Soap, who do not croon themselves to sleep at night with lullabies including the words Bits and Bytes and Fifth Generation. Not only do the engineers not speak, or think, in English, they also have priorities which don't include explaining their gadgetry to end users. (That's what they call the people who will eventually employ their inventions.)

In order to interest potential end-users, advertisements have to be written. If that interest is to become more than a passing fancy, publicity handouts have to be put together to explain the benefits of the technology and how it would work in the client's business. If the client decides to invest, he or she must go away with a set of manuals that will explain how to implement particular processes on the computer, and will establish a procedure by which a fault can be diagnosed and resolved. All of this material must be in ordinary English. It must be accessible, preferably interesting and ideally it should be lively and personal. People who can turn out this kind of writing are in considerable demand, and it is a demand which is growing.

If you decide to do high-tech writing, then two considerations are paramount. The first is that you must cost your time, not your output. Look at it this way. The manual my friend eventually produced was twenty-two printed pages in length. It was laid out in foolproof steps, each indented and printed on a separated line. *War and Peace* it wasn't. But it took an enormous commitment of time because of the initial understanding of the technology, then the writing of the instructions, and finally, the double-checking of each instruction to make sure that, followed, it always delivered the same result. If you are to make a living or part of a living at high tech writing, then you must make sure that you are paid for the *process* by which the end result is achieved, rather than the word-count of that end result.

The other consideration is confidentiality. If a computer manufacturer sits you down with its soft-ware engineers, or gives you access to internal documentation about design and development, you will learn a lot more than will appear in the manual you have been commissioned to write. Some of what you will learn will be highly confidential. It is important to indicate your understanding of that confidentiality to the client. Some companies have a contract which covers this. Read it carefully and make sure that it does not limit your capacity to do similar confidential work for other information technology houses in a way that would damage your prospects.

Local Radio

Moving on to other growing markets, one of the most obvious is that of local radio. These days, small is beautiful when it comes to radio stations. Because of that factor of scale, fees are not enormous. But a regular supply of small cheques makes your bank manager just as happy as an irregular supply of larger cheques.

In Britain and Ireland, the number of small stations does not compare with those available as a market in the US. Nevertheless, local radio is going to be a more important outlet for writers in the next ten years than it ever has been in the past.

The growth in local radio is directly paralleled by the growth in specialist publications. One of the major trends, internationally, in the world of magazines, has been the division of the mass market into countless smaller, "niche" markets. Great big glossy magazines with massive readership numbers which, twenty years ago looked invulnerable, have folded. Yet the magazine racks in corner shops have, if anything, become larger and more crowded. For every big publication that has gone under, a dozen smaller, more precisely targeted publications have sprung up. On my desk as I write is:

- A magazine about skateboarding
- Amagazine about low-impact aerobics
- A magazine about environmental issues
- A magazine about small businesses
- A magazine about personal computers
- A magazine about retirement
- A magazine about house-swapping

None of these existed ten years ago. Each meets the needs of a precise market, and delivers to advertisers an equally precise readership. So when an advertiser wants to reach retired people in order to sell them "golden years" holidays, he does not have to spend a fortune on advertising in big, general magazines in the hope of reaching this particular audience; he can hit a nail on the head most cost-effectively.

Each of these specialist magazines offers a market for writers who can tailor their material.

CVs and Academic editing

Good exam results and a civil letter of application rarely win jobs these days. The curriculum vitae is a pre requisite. Even though most people are familiar with the details of their own academic and work life to date, this familiarity, of itself, does not qualify them to do a good CV. Quite apart from the capacity to do a subtle but effective selling job on themselves, many of them do not have the typewriter or typing skills to produce a visually impressive personal statement.

The creation, typing and presentation of CVs is a very special skill. It is time-consuming, and the best appearance results from the best typing technology; a laser-printed CV looks a lot better than one cobbled together on your Uncle Mike's senile Underwood with the ghostly ribbon. If you decide to do CVs, then you must plan to spend time with the person for whom you are doing the job. In effect, what you are producing is a Personality Profile (page 77) which is relentlessly on the sunny side of the street. A good CV is much more than tombstone details. It must give the flavour of the person who is presenting herself or himself for consideration.

Ideally, it should be created in response to the particular job description and it should take into account the public profile and corporate culture of the potential employer. This means that a general CV is of limited value. The best CV services I know are those operated by writers who own word processors which can store a template version of someone's CV. This can be edited to gear it for a particular job and a fresh hard copy fed out each time. In my view, it is unacceptable to send a CV which has handwritten additions and emendations on it. The inference is easily drawn that this applicant does not greatly value himself or herself, and certainly does not value the organisation to which application is being made.

Costing this service is difficult. It takes time. It is quite difficult to do really well. Therefore it should pay well. Unfortunately, it is a growing market dogged by the presence of willing amateurs who are prepared to "fling something together" for half-nothing. Once a professional has been doing CVs successfully for a few months, the track record is there for quotation in support of a good price.

"It's going to cost you £120," the CV expert says calmly. "Yes, I know your cousin can type it up for you for a few quid, but my service is much more than a typing service. My CVs get people jobs. They do that because I put time and expertise into them, and that costs £120."

Selling this service can be done by listing in the commercial telephone directories, a notice in public areas of universities and other colleges, an advertisement in student periodicals read by final year students, by mail shot, word of mouth and frequently-dropped business cards.

Much the same applies to thesis doctoring and presentation. In the past decade, there seems to have been an explosion in the number of final year students of all disciplines who must produce theses in order to gain their diploma or degree. Frequently, they do the research and the bones of the text but have no idea how to present the material. If there are rules about the organisation of graphs, footnotes and so on, the writers of today's theses don't know about them. In some cases, tutors give out sheets which provide skeletal guidelines, but for the most part, theses are like buckets of popcorn; you can't quite see where it has all come from, there is no particular shape to it, and the task of getting through it is welcome or unwelcome depending on the personal hunger of the reader.

The best how-to book on dissertations and theses that I have come upon is one published fifty years ago, but continuously in print since then. Called *A Manual for Writers of Term Papers, Theses and Dissertations,* it went into its fifth edition in 1987. The author is Kate L. Turaban, and it was published by the University of Chicago Press. There is now an English edition published by Heinemann of London at £6.95 Sterling.

This chapter looks at the most obvious of the growing markets at this particular point. There are others. There always are. And, if you're prepared to obey a few do's and don'ts, you can make money exploiting those markets.

DON'TS

- *Don't* look down on any market. If people want to read it, then it's worth doing and it's worth doing well.

- *Don't* be half-hearted about a new market. Investing time can facilitate your later delivery of what that market really needs at a price it is prepared to pay.

- *Don't* expect a market to present or define itself. Diamonds and other precious things have to be mined.

- *Don't* go overboard into any one growing market. That way lies burnout. CVs may keep starvation at bay, but doing nothing other than CVs will drive a writer around the twist.

- *Don't* overstretch your visibility. If Annie Other writes speeches, press releases, CVs, romantic novels and booklets on freestyle leaping from bridges, putting her name on all of them devalues them, gives her the public image of a promiscuous workaholic, and confuses the hell out of the buying public.

DOS

- *Do* enjoy the variety offered by different kinds of writing. One swallow may not make a summer, but it makes a heck of a nice break after a few hundred sparrows. The Great Novel is easier to return to when you have whipped up a fast romantic souffle over a week or so.

- *Do* keep your eyes and ears open. The world runs on words. Somebody is usually writing those words, often for money. Why shouldn't that somebody be you?

- *Do* "Market by Wandering About." Be seen to be accessible and available for writing assignments.

- *Do* concentrate on "line extension." If you write small DIY pieces for your local paper, could you do three minute inputs to a radio programme? Or present an audio cassette tape for the Christmas market? Or provide a timber company with giveaway leaflets?

- *Do* solve other people's problems. Think about what you can offer which will allow a newspaper or publication to gain more advertising or readership, and then explain the benefit to them of buying your service.

Chapter 12

Making a Living

A living is made by selling something that everybody needs at least once a year. Yes, sir.

And a million is made by producing something that everybody needs every day. You artists produce something that nobody needs at any time.

Thornton Wilder

- I'd like to give up my job and write full time, but how do you know when you're at that stage of development?

- Being published is what matters, not what you get paid for being published.

- How can you be sure that a publisher is not robbing you?

- How badly are writers hit by income tax?

- Do you need to have an accountant if you're a writer?

Writers are supposed to be above earthly considerations like budgets. It's part of their image. They think on higher things, so you don't have to pay them much. Let's face it, they all live in garrets, don't they? And how much does your average garret cost to rent or buy?

Why writers should value themselves by proportion to their level of commercial ignorance, I don't know. But that's the way it is. If you can't read a balance sheet, if you can't balance your income against your expenditure, and if the idea of setting a yearly income target puts your teeth on edge, then, according to the popular myth, you must be a truly talented writer.

Rubbish.

Most writers who start off innocent end up poor or embittered or both. They end up poor because they never manage to earn enough money to live from their writing, and they end up embittered because they handle money and contracts badly. Too often, a writer who is so grateful for the chance of publication that he pays no attention to the contract subsequently resents the terms he agreed and the thousands he feels he lost as a result.

If you want to be an artistic amateur, then you must skip the rest of this chapter. If you want to be a money-earning professional, then there are a number of steps you need to take from the very beginning of your writing career. The first is putting a value on your work.

There are lots of different approaches to this. You can seek information from the National Union of Journalists about freelance rates. This will give you some idea as to what amount of money newspapers or magazines are prepared to pay for 600 or 1,000 words.

The only problem about this approach is that what the NUJ has managed to negotiate for its freelance members has two strings attached to it. The first string is that it applies *to its members*. If you are not a member of the union, then you are on your own, and liable to meet with a derisive laugh if you quote union rates to an editor who knows you to be a newcomer. The second string is that the freelance rate stated by the NUJ is always a minimum. It is the rate below which no union man or woman should work. Consequently, it is on the low side, and it is never good to set your sights below what is possible.

The great difficulty about writers deciding on their worth is that so much of their creative and analytical power goes on other things. I have found that when I ask a group of talented newcomers what they'd like to earn as writers, they get all shifty with embarrassment, until one of them decides to be hard-nosed and say, with decisive indecision "Well, I'd like to make a *decent living*." Everybody nods. When asked to define a decent living and confusion breaks out among the group. If members of the group are women who have been out of the paid workforce for a few years they are baffled by the logistics of costing their time; nobody in our society puts a money value on having and rearing kids, tending the sick and creating a home.

If you are in this position, play a little money game with yourself. Envisage yourself at a party, one year from now. Somebody has asked you what you do for a living, and you control the surge of pride inside yourself long enough to say, understatedly, "I'm a writer." (Work hard at what this book suggests, and you will have no problem, one year from today, in saying precisely that.) Now, imagine that somebody at the party doesn't really know that you are a serious writer, and asks if you can make money at it. (They won't, but play the game to its conclusion.) "I don't know about other people," you say. "But I plan to make £12,000 next year." The figure does not matter. It could be £20,000. It could be £6,000. What is important is that you decide, right now, what your target is, and then work out the details of how to reach it.

Targets depend on tax. If you plan to write a massive internationally bestselling novel which will sell to the movies and be a Book Club Offering in addition to its inclusion in shortened form in the *Reader's Digest*, and if you live in Ireland, then you can set your target at £50,000 for the coming year, and if you can prove to the Irish Exchequer that your work is of artistic merit, that £50,000 will be yours, in toto. No tax. The Irish tax concession, designed to facilitate artists, is one of the reasons why novelists like Richard Condon and Len Deighton have spent years living away from their countries of origin.

It's a great tax concession. But it only applies to works of art. So if you plan to research and write a tome about the location and physical state of each and every wreck from the Spanish Armada, and if it becomes a bestseller, then, even in Ireland a goodly chunk of tax will be taken out of the monies earned.

"But that's not *fair*," I hear you cry. "There's much more work involved in researching a factual book than in just writing fiction off the top of your head."

Fair or not fair, the situation is that Ireland is one of the most tax-efficient countries to live in, if you are writing fiction, poetry or drama. If you are writing fact-based material then, no matter what time it takes to research, what you get paid will be taxed.

The reason I suggest this games-playing exercise of imagining yourself being asked questions about your profession and your earnings is that one of the techniques used with a high degree of success in many countries when it comes to the training of athletes is what's called "envisaging." Athletes who, in advance of a race, "see" the stages of the event in their mind's eye tend to do better than those who have not gone through the procedures. Whenever you face a challenge, it is worth sitting down and envisaging how you will handle it. Whenever you have a foggy ambition, envisaging yourself answering questions about it will help you define the limits of that ambition.

So, let us assume that you have decided to opt for a target for the coming year of £10,000. You're not going to work every day of the year. (It may be that you *should* work every day of the year, but few of us do.) So you want to take Saturday and Sunday off? OK, I'll give you Saturday and Sunday. 52 of each in any year. That's 104 days off. Plus 3 weeks of working days off. Plus another five days off for when you get mumps, measles, mange, or any combination of the three. Plus another five days for bank holidays. And another five for luck. That leaves you with 230 working days every year.

Now divide your target—£10,000, remember—by the number of days available to you. 230 goes into £10,000 exactly 43.478 times. Which means that you must earn 43 pounds and 48 pence every one of those working days. That in turn means that every hour is worth about a fiver to you.

Let us assume that you are asked to write a feature for a magazine that you know is going to take a day for research and another half day for writing. Quite apart from any direct expenses incurred in the project (which might include telephone calls and petrol) this means that you must make £65 on it. If you are to meet your target.

The problem is that if you plan to earn money by contributing to newspapers and magazines, you are not in a position as a newcomer, to catch an editor by the short and curlies and suggest that he should pay you your chosen fee or else. If, for that day and a half of work, he is happy to pay you £50 but would be reduced to despondency by a demand for £65, then you would be well advised to take the 50. Take it and note it, because if you want to join the NUJ they will require documentation to prove that your claimed earnings are real. In the early stages of a writing career, you have to work harder for less money than you may be able to demand later on.

Realistically, you will need to have placed a few features with publications and seen the kind of money they are prepared to offer you, before you can do the sums and come up with a realistic target for yourself. One woman I know started writing in her mid-thirties and, faced with the proposal that she should set herself a financial target, decided, in her first year to try for £3,000. At the end of that year, she had made £4,300, but had decided that in the following year, not only would she double her income, but that she would make more profit.

"Some of the jobs I was doing were taking me half a week to get through," she told me. "And others were taking me a couple of hours, yet they were paying the same."

Her only problem was pulling out of the weekly job which was costing more to do than it was earning her.

"It takes a full day to do the research," she said. "I start at eight in the morning, and I rarely get finished before four thirty. I do an average of thirty two miles, and I have to make six phone calls. Because it all has to be done within one day, I sometimes have to park illegally and so I get a ticket about once a month.

"The next day, I have to do all the calculations, write the text, have someone else check out all the tots and ensure that my copy matches the figures, and then, because it's a very tight deadline, I have to drive in and leave it literally on the editor's desk."

For this, she was being paid thirty quid.

"Why haven't you asked for more?" I queried.

"I don't think I really could," she said shamefacedly. "And anyway, I was talking to another freelance who works for him, and she said nobody ever gets more than thirty and I should consider myself lucky."

"Hold it right there," I said. "Don't discuss your earnings with other writers. Especially freelances. We all try to be supportive, but it bugs the hell out of me if I think you are doing better than me, and if you're not, it makes me very comfortable and I'd be just as happy to see you stay in that situation. So don't talk to other writers. Keep your earnings to yourself, unless you get into a situation where collective action against an exploitative editor is indicated. Now, why can't you talk to the editor?"

"I'd be embarrassed."

"Why?"

"I don't know. I just... he'd think I was getting above myself. If he thought the job was worth more, he'd have paid me more."

"Editors pay as little as they can get away with. That's why they're in management. Newspapers and magazines set out to make a profit, and editors whose freelances are coming in dripping mink don't usually make a profit."

The notion of her particular editor as a factor in the decidedly black bottom line of his newspaper's annual report did not sit easily in my friend's mind. He was far too pleasant and friendly to be interested in nasty things like profit.

"I doubt it," I said. "But let's go back to what you said about him paying you more for the job if he thought it was worth more. Did you inherit this job from somebody else?"

A shake of the head greeted this. She had come up with a new concept and pitched it at the editor when they were strangers to each other. He had bought it.

"Did you have any idea how much work would be involved when you proposed it to him?"

Another shake of the head.

"How long ago was that?"

After much mental arithmetic, she worked out that it was eight months.

"So he sent you thirty quid the first week and thirty quid has passed through your letter box every week since?"

A nod this time.

"For starters," I said, "there's every chance that the payment has recurred like a repeat prescription ever since, and that he now hasn't a clue what he's paying you because it is not something he has actively to decide about each week. But let's get over to his side and look at its value to him. How often has he rejected it?"

She goggled at me. Never had the piece been rejected. The idea was so startling to her that I could see her developing retrospective anxiety about submissions that had probably deserved rejection.

"Is it popular?"

Oh, yes, she said. Oh, definitely. It created a minor controversy every week and letters to the editor and a daily radio programme never failed to mention it the morning it appeared.

"And it's really solid," she said with sudden enthusiasm. "Whenever there has been a query about any of the facts given, I've been able to give chapter and verse. I've never, ever been caught out and he really likes that."

"That's where you start your negotiations from," I told her. "You drop in one day to him and you tell him how much you enjoy doing this job and what a high it gives you to know that he relies on you to get the facts absolutely straight. The only thing is that when he gave you your big break eight months ago, you didn't know, and you're quite sure he didn't know how much work would be involved in researching and double-checking the figures each week. Now that it has been running a while you have been able to do the costs, and you would be very grateful if he would talk to the accountancy people about getting the fee to about £65, with perhaps a tenner for expenses."

"I was just thinking of telling him I'd be happy to train in somebody else to do it," she said.

Bad idea, I told her. It would imply that she had got tired of a job, not that it was worth more money. It would also imply that any fool could do this particular job. If she followed the lines I suggested, she was underlining the value of the job to the editor, stitching him as part-originator, removing any potential guilt attributable to him as a mean payer, and giving him data on paper he could use to justify paying his writer more.

"Mentioning the accountants is always a good idea," I told her. "In theory, then, you're not fighting directly with an editor you're telling him you know he has an awful time with these difficult number-cruncher people. And in reality, he will genuinely have to defend a sudden radical increase in the money paid, so you're giving him these figures on paper allows him to say to his purse-string people 'look, this is what it costs to have a guarantee—if you want to go for a cheaper job, don't blame me if we end up in court being sued by someone on the basis of our printing inaccurate figures'."

When the writer went to this particular editor, she had a fraught meeting, not because he undervalued what she was doing, but because more than doubling the amount paid would play hell with his budgets. He eventually came to a complicated compromise whereby she got paid something like £47 for the job, £9 for expenses and £267 for retrospective expenses. They agreed that three months from then, the basic fees would go to £60 and the expenses to £15. Three years later, she is still doing the job, and when I asked her what she's now being paid, she smiled sweetly and refused to tell me.

"Someone once advised me not to tell other freelances what I was making," she said reflectively. "So I won't tell you. But I'm doing OK, thank you. I haven't doubled my income every year, but I'm certainly making three times, this year, the £3,000 I had planned to make in my first year."

Getting the mix right is fundamental. If you're on the staff of a wealthy national newspaper, then, assuming you come across a suppurating scandal somewhere, there is a chance that you will be allowed to allocate days, if not weeks of time to that story. If you are a freelance, paying for serious bread, milk and tea out of your earnings, you cannot afford to get bogged down in just one story which may pay you well after six weeks. The people who do best out of freelance magazine and newspaper writing are those who do a little bit of everything.

Writer A
Has a monthly horoscope feature in a glossy magazine, two scripts a week for a radio programme, and a research job that takes half a day. They are the staples. Around them she builds a series of money-earning, but not regular, jobs.

Writer B
Does two nights' subbing for a weekly newspaper, has a sports column and does CVs on the side. In addition, he writes profiles of the rich and famous for magazines in his home country and overseas.

Writer C
Writes a computer piece for a Sunday newspaper, provides a humorous column for his own local newspaper, does sports reporting at the weekend, and is halfway through a factual book for which he got an advance of £500.

Doing a variety of writing jobs makes commercial sense. Jobs which pay only a small amount of money must be balanced by the big payers, and jobs which take a lot of time and expense by pieces which, although they are backed by years of experience, can be put together in a couple of hours at the typewriter.

Willingness to negotiate with an editor, and competence in that negotiation, can mean the difference between making a good living and being in a constant financial turmoil. A few hints on negotiating better money out of editors:

Be realistic
As an editor and director of a small publishing house, I ran into

trouble with a writer who wanted an advance of £2,000 for her book. Her opening statement was that if we wanted to publish her book—and we did—that was the price of it. My opening statement was to close the file and give her the name of a much bigger publishing house. There was simply no way a small publishing house could ever have divvied up such an advance. Similarly, your local community newsletter can never match *Cosmopolitan* in payment for a feature.

Don't negotiate on the phone
If possible, do it in person. Real live human beings are much less dismissable than voices on the phone.

Never complain about the past
You don't want an admission of past meanness. You want future generosity.

Think about it from his point of view
What's the benefit to him of paying you more money? Does it allow you to devote more time to his job? Does it give him the exclusive use of your name? Does it give him an item he would not like to see going to a competitor? If there is no benefit to an editor in paying you more, then all you have going for you, as a freelance, is his sense of natural justice.

Time it
Editors hate continuing nags. Negotiate once a year and then shut up.

Establish your personal bottom line before you start
If he says "forget it," what are you going to do? Deciding in advance what is the worst scenario and planning for it will prevent panic setting in halfway through a negotiation. Think it through. He says "forget it." Do you then say "OK I won't work for you any more," or have you talked to alternative employers? The simultaneous throwing out of babies and bathwater can be emotionally satisfying, but it is a short-lived

expensive thrill. Even if you plan, long-term, to take your wonders elsewhere if he won't pay up, work out in advance a method of hanging on to his job in the short-term. Smile and smile and be a solvent villain.

Gift wrap the negotiation

Bring twelve new ideas to be discussed at the same time. Otherwise the next time you seek a meeting with him, he will recall only that the last time you were looking for money, and his enthusiasm for a further meeting will be just a touch muted.

Negotiation with a newspaper editor is one thing. Negotiation with a book publisher is quite a different thing. When a publishing house tells you what you have written is worth publishing and that they will issue it a year later, the euphoria induced is such that if they put a contract in front of you which had, in its small print, a provision entitling them to thinly slice, deep fry and bag your granny for sale in local delis, you would smilingly sign it.

All relationships between writers and publishers start with exultant commitment. Thereafter, the go the same way marriages do. Some mature into mutual respect and happy productivity. Some end up in divorce and litigation about the details of soured goodwill. It is, accordingly, no insult to a publisher to read a contract very carefully, to seek legal or other advice on it, and to negotiate changes if the base document does not meet the writer's requirements.

Developing and maintaining a good relationship with clients is an essential part of a professional writer's life. As is managing money. As a writer, you will develop your own system, but it is important that you have a system which keeps account of what you have written for which publication, when it was sent, when you checked up on its progress, whether it was accepted or rejected, and (assuming a rejection) where you sent it thereafter. The system should take account of the expenses involved in each job, and the payment eventually received so that you can analyse once a quarter which jobs are financially worthwhile and which are not. It may be that, having analysed your earnings, you decide to keep doing some job which has no profit level because it brings some advantage, whether that be visibility in a prestigious publication or a sense of fellowship with the people involved, but it is nonetheless important that you do not fool yourself that you are making a living out of something which is no more than a personal indulgence.

Depending on the tax laws at any given time, it may suit you very well to have some of your payments made out as "expenses," rather than to receive a single cheque from a publication. One way or the other, keep fanatical accounts of everything which can be attributed as a cost to the exercise of your profession. A writer of apparently spontaneous poetic novels was the first to explain this to me.

"I get a tax rebate on my typewriter, my ribbons, my power going into the back of the machine," he told me. "I keep accounts of every pen I buy, every bottle of Tipp-Ex, every package of paper, every phone call I have to make. This year, I'm going to buy a new carpet for the study I write in, and by God I'm going to take the price to the Revenue Commissioners to see if they'll give me anything because the old carpet got worn away through my pacing up and down on it whenever I was stuck."

When I pointed out to him that as an Irish resident, although his country of origin was not Irish, he was entitled to pay no tax on his earnings from novels anyway, he pointed out that he had to pay tax on other writing and that anything which mitigated the amount of tax to be paid, without wasting his good writing time, was worth doing.

Whether or not you should have an accountant is up to you.

Writing is a business. Setting targets and systems for coping with the finances and administration can free a writer to get on with the central task—getting words on paper.

DON'TS

- *Don't* be vague about the living you want to earn. Setting a target gives you something to aim for.

- *Don't* assume that editors will value your work less if you ask them to pay you adequately for it. Nobody values what they get free of charge.

- *Don't* whinge. If you lose a round with an editor, and have your request for more money refused, either stop working for him or get on with it and make another energetic attempt after a decent interval.

- *Don't* lose documentation about expenses.

- *Don't* spend too much time on financial matters. You are a writer, not a book keeper.

DOS

- *Do* regard administration as a legitimate part of your career skills.

- *Do* develop systems for tracking what you have written and what payments you have received.

- *Do* take income tax seriously. Confine your creativity to your manuscripts.

- *Do* seek professional help. But get very good references which ensure that the professional you use knows about writers and publishers.

- *Do* read all contracts and establish professional, rather than merely friendly, relationships with publishers and other clients. Goodwill can evaporate very quickly.

General Reading about Writers and Writing

E. Cobham Brewer L.L.D., *The Dictionary of Phrase and Fable* (New York 1981)

Rita Mae Brown, *Starting From Scratch* (New York 1988)

Fredrick Busch, *When People Publish* (Iowa 1986)

Brenda Euland, *If You Want to Write* (New York 1938)

E.M. Forster, *Aspects of the Novel* (London 1927)

Stephen Fox, *The Mirror Makers* (New York 1984)

Robert Graves, *The Crowning Privilege* (London 1955)

Sir Ernest Gowers, *The Complete Plain Words* (London 1954)

Stephen Klaidman/Tom L. Beauchamp, *The Virtuous Journalist* (New York 1987)

Norman Longmate, *Writing for the BBC* (London 1977)

Peter Schwed Macmillan *Turning The Pages* (New York 1985)

Eric Partridge, *A Dictionary of Cliches* (London 1940)

William C. Paxson, *The Business Writing* (New York)

Harry Porter, *Lies, Damned Lies* (London 1984)

Anthony Storr, *The Dynamics of Creation* (London 1972)

David Weir and Dan Moyes, *Raising Hell* (Massachusetts 1983)

Tom Wolfe & E.W. Johnson, *The New Journalism* (London 1975)

The Penguin International Thesaurus of Quotations.

Writers Market
An annual directory to markets for articles, books, jokes, greeting cards, novels, plays and short stories, produced in America. Useful if you plan to market your work overseas, and obtainable by mail order from:

Writer's Digest
Subscriber Service Dept.
205 West Centre Street
Marion, Ohio 43306-0001

From the same address, you can have mailed to you a monthly magazine called *Writer's Digest,* which costs about £15 for twelve monthly issues.

POOLBEG

Also published by Poolbeg

Just a Few Words

All You Need to Know about
Speaking in Public

by
Terry Prone

How to deliver a speech,
make a presentation
or give an interview for radio and television,
and much, much more.

£4.99